# LONG ROAD TO BOSTON

## The Pursuit of the World's Most Coveted Marathon

By Mark Sutcliffe

Great River Media Inc.

# ABOUT THE AUTHOR

Mark Sutcliffe is the author of *Why I Run: The Remarkable Journey of the Ordinary Runner* and *Canada's Magnificent Marathon*. As the founder, publisher and back-page columnist of *iRun* magazine, and the host of its radio show and podcast, Mark has been sharing the stories of ordinary and elite runners for more than a decade.

When he's not running, Mark is an entrepreneur, broadcaster and writer in his hometown of Ottawa, Canada. He hosts a daily talk show on 1310 NEWS and writes weekly in the *Ottawa Citizen*, where he was previously executive editor. Mark is a passionate volunteer who has led several community organizations and has raised almost $200,000 with charity runs.

Mark lives in Ottawa with his wife Ginny and their children, Erica, Jack and Kate. *Long Road to Boston* is his fifth book. The 2015 Boston Marathon was Mark's twenty-second marathon.

Great River Media, 2016


Published in Canada by Great River Media, Inc. Ottawa in 2016

$29.95 in Canada and $24.95 in the US

ISBN: 978-0-9868242-8-9
*Long Road to Boston* (bound)

ISBN: 978-0-9868242-9-6
*Long Road to Boston* (electronic book)

Manuscript edited by Kel Pero

Cover illustration: Sarah Lazarovic

Design and production: Tanya Connolly-Holmes

Great River Media
Suite 500 - 250 City Centre Avenue
Ottawa, ON
K1R 6K7

greatriver.ca

Printed in Canada

When I run, I wear Mizuno. I wear Mizuno shoes. I wear Mizuno shirts and shorts. I wear Mizuno hats. When it's cold, I wear a Mizuno Breath Thermo jacket and Mizuno gloves. Whether I'm at the start of the Boston Marathon or on a routine run through my neighbourhood, you won't see me in any other gear. (Yes, that's one of my Mizuno shoes on the cover of this book.)

Like the television commercial about tires, it's important for runners to remember that the only thing that makes contact with the road is your footwear. So if you want to run well and reduce the risk of injuries, there's nothing more important. Mizuno shoes are unlike any other shoe I have worn. They combine unique Wave technology with unparalleled expertise in producing shoes that fit well and support your running. And their gear is always comfortable and stylish.

But what I like about Mizuno is not just that they make great products, but that they're into running and they're into runners. They live and breathe the sport and they engage runners all over North America and listen to their feedback.

Thanks to Mizuno for sponsoring me as a runner and for supporting *Long Road to Boston* as the lead sponsor. Mizuno has been with me every step of the way for thousands of miles.

# WIGWAM

For almost as long as there has been a Boston Marathon, Wigwam Mills has been making socks. The company was founded in 1905 in Sheboygan, Wisconsin, and they continue to knit their products there to this day. Unlike so many other manufacturers, they haven't shipped production overseas, and they are dedicated to working with and supporting domestic suppliers. They are focused on quality, honesty, and integrity, and they genuinely care about their customers.

I wear Wigwam when I run because they make terrific socks. I put in a lot of miles, and I've tried many other socks that can't keep up. They get beat up quickly and show wear and tear almost immediately. Wigwam socks are incredibly durable and extremely comfortable. I'm grateful to Wigwam for their sponsorship of *Long Road to Boston*.

You won't be surprised that I use a lot of running analogies when I'm talking about other subjects. Nowhere is that more appropriate than when I recommend the approach of PWL Capital.

I've been a PWL Capital client for more than a decade. Investing for the future is a lot like training for a marathon: there are no shortcuts. A lot of people will try to convince you that they have some magical strategy to get great returns on the stock market, but that's like saying there's a trick that can get you from the couch to a marathon in just a few days.

Like most things in life, the rewards of both investing and running come from smart, long-term hard work that is supported by evidence. That's the approach I take to my training, and it's the proven method PWL Capital uses on behalf of its investing clients. They don't subscribe to fads or schemes.

Thanks to the folks at PWL Capital in Ottawa for sponsoring *Long Road to Boston*. Like marathon runners, they're all about the long run.

There are a lot of people in the running business who try to sell solutions. The people at SoleFit, a pedorthic clinic in Ottawa, always figure out the problem first. I've worked with them on a number of occasions, and talked to many other runners who've had the same experience.

SoleFit does gait analysis and makes custom orthotics, along with helping clients with knee bracing and other recovery products. But their knowledge goes much deeper than that. They understand biomechanics and technique, and they're up-to-date on all the latest footwear. And they're runners, so they understand runners.

SoleFit supports runners by looking at the entire picture. They try to figure out the source of the problem rather than push a quick solution on a client. And they try not just to treat issues, but to prevent them from reoccurring. Thanks to the great people at SoleFit for supporting *Long Road to Boston*.

# THANK YOU!

I'm eternally grateful to the following people who supported *Long Road to Boston* through a crowdfunding campaign. It's deeply gratifying to have the backing of a community of kind and generous individuals.

Beth Agro
Doug Baum
Lynda Bordeleau
Jason Brazeau
Catherine Cano
Neale and Allyson Chisnall
David Coletto
Julie Drury
Barry Dworkin
Barbara Farber
Brent Ferguson
Lisa Georges
Stéphane Giguère
Nancy Graham
Dan Greenberg
Bruce Hillary
Dennis Jackson
Scott Johnson
Jack Kitts
David Luxton
Ida Mikhael
Alex Munter
Rick O'Shaughnessy
Donna Roney
Colin Rowe
Marc Roy
Aaron Rubinoff
Brent Smyth
Jane Spiteri
Louisa Taylor
Anathea Théorêt
Gene Villeneuve
Shirley and John Westeinde
Patrick Whalen
Vern White
David Willson

# TABLE OF CONTENTS

# FOREWORD

By Bart Yasso

The course of the Boston Marathon hasn't changed very much over the past one hundred and twenty years. Hundreds of thousands of runners have left Hopkinton and have moved in almost a straight line, with only a handful of turns, to Boylston Street in Copley Square. When the gun goes off, we all travel the same path to the finish line.

But each one of those runners takes a different route to get to the start line. What prompts all of us first to do a marathon, then to strive for and achieve a qualifying time, then actually to run the Boston Marathon? I've talked to thousands of Boston runners over the past thirty-five years, and every story is different.

I first ran Boston in 1982, the year of the famous "duel in the sun" between Alberto Salazar and Dick Beardsley. On my first visit, I spent a lot of time before the race walking around the city, and discovered first-hand what so many people had told me about the atmosphere on marathon weekend. As soon as people find out you're a runner, they want to know where you're from and every detail about your story. Wherever you go that weekend, people are talking about the marathon.

Since then, I've been to Boston every single Patriots' Day, a few times as a runner but mostly in my capacity as Chief Running Officer of *Runner's World*. I've seen the race transform from a fairly small event populated by very fast athletes into an enormous spectacle that has become the ultimate goal for the everyday runner.

What makes the Boston Marathon special is its unparalleled history. It's not the most picturesque marathon course in the world. It's not run at the best time of year; the weather can be very unpredictable.

But what no other event can match is the one-hundred and twenty years of tradition. There are runners who have been back every year for decades. There are families who have shown up to the same location as spectators every year for generations. Because the race is run on a holiday, it's like a party on the streets.

The race has changed, but the tradition hasn't. Thirty years ago, a small group of runners gathered every April in tiny Hopkinton. Now it's a field in the tens of thousands. The first few years I ran Boston, there were spectators edging onto the course; by the time you got to Commonwealth Avenue, it was so narrow in some places that runners were traveling almost in single file. If you wanted to pass someone, you had to tap him or her on the shoulder and ask him or her to move over. Now it's a highly organized, professionally run event run by an extraordinary team. Once upon a time, when you got to the finish line, you got the time that was on the clock when you crossed. Now there's a sophisticated chip timing system, one of many technological improvements to racing.

What also hasn't changed over the decades is the passion of the runners who seek an invitation to run Boston. Every year, I'm amazed by the stories of people who have made the Boston Marathon the most important item on their bucket list, the pinnacle of their running career. Some people train for years just to get in. The qualifying standards are a big part of the appeal: runners know that it's not a free ticket. You have to earn the right to a bib number in Boston.

Mark's story is a perfect example. He's been running marathons for more than a decade and started getting closer to qualifying in his sixteenth marathon. Like so many other runners, he didn't give up. I admire the commitment, persistence and determination of all the runners who have made Boston a significant goal in their lives. I never get tired of meeting the runners who are doing Boston for the first time and seeing how much it means to them. In my experience, the most amazing stories are in Boston, because runners have gone through so much sacrifice just to get there.

The Boston Marathon continues to be a magical event I look forward to every year. This book captures exactly why it's the most prestigious and most cherished race on the planet.

*"Running is a big question mark that's there each and every day. It asks you: Are you going to be a wimp or are you going to be strong today?"*

**PETER MAHER**

# PROLOGUE

*May 18, 2014*

It's the final mile of the Poconos Run for the Red Marathon in Stroudsberg, Pennsylvania, and I am still on pace to achieve the goal I've been working toward for years: to run the fastest marathon of my life and qualify for the world's most coveted race, the Boston Marathon.

But there's a problem, sneaking up on me like footsteps from behind: my calf muscles are gradually starting to seize up. It is, lamentably, a familiar development: this has happened to me in at least five other marathons and it rarely ends well. It starts with an occasional twinge every few minutes, harmless but ominous. Once in a while, if I'm lucky, it doesn't escalate from there. More often, though, it steadily intensifies until there is a painful, debilitating and soul-crushing spasm every time my foot strikes the pavement. In one race, even after I stopped running and started walking, the contractions were so intense and incapacitating that I almost fell over.

I dread this possibility in every marathon. No matter how smoothly the race is being run, the backs of my legs are always in the back of my mind. *Will it happen? How soon? And how bad will it get?*

Here in Pennsylvania, it's still manageable, but my stride is changing from a solid, controlled pace to a quick, desperate shuffle. I feel like Lightning McQueen in the opening scene of my son's favorite movie, Cars, hopping frantically toward the checkered flag with two flat tires and a pair of challengers bearing down on him. How long will it be before I am walking or stumbling, watching the minutes pass me by like faster runners, until my goal is lost one more time?

As I've learned from experience, no matter how well you are doing halfway or even farther into a marathon, you can never be optimistic until you see the finish line. You can run a great race for 20 miles, then blow it all if your legs or your energy give out. It's like mounting an incredible comeback in a championship basketball game, standing at the free-throw line with a chance to sink the go-ahead points, and watching your shots clunk off the rim like bricks. A marathon can create such fulfilment and validation, but when it falls apart, it can shatter the spirit. You slow down or stop while the rest of the field slips past you, vanishing into the distance along with your dreams.

I haven't completely given up hope. But then I'm struck by what seems to be the decisive blow. The pace bunny for my Boston-qualifying time of three hours and twenty-five minutes zooms past me on my right. Traveling at a prescribed pace, he is the personification of my target; success or failure comes down to whether I finish ahead of or behind him. For twenty-five miles I have stayed a safe distance in front of him, but now he is disappearing down the road ahead. Like time, the pace bunny waits for no one. He has chased me down and left me in his wake.

*It's over*, I think to myself. Yet another failed attempt. Once again I've trained for months, running six times a week, doing speed work and long runs, eating (mostly) the right foods and managing my weight. Once again I've left my family behind to travel to a race that is supposed to have favorable conditions for a fast result. Once again I will return empty-handed. I feel like Homer Simpson thinking he will cross Springfield Gorge on a skateboard – *I'm going to make it!* – only to fall suddenly short of the target and tumble perilously down the cliff.

It has been a long journey – and I'm not referring to the last twenty-five miles. For as long as I can remember, even before I started running, I've wanted to do the Boston Marathon. For six years, it's been a stated objective. And for the past four marathons, my only focus has been to finish in a time fast enough to qualify for the oldest and most cherished marathon on the planet. For more than two years I've trained exclusively for one reason, some five or six hundred runs covering four thousand miles, with only one thing on my mind.

And I've come agonizingly close. In my last race, I was twenty-two seconds from the goal, less than one second per mile. My results in training have told me that a Boston-qualifying time is within my grasp. And yet I can't seem to pull everything together when it counts. Something always goes wrong and I miss the target. The pattern seems to be repeating itself in this, my twentieth marathon.

I'm not sure how much more of this I can take. I stop running and start walking. And I begin to think about what I will tell my wife and all those who believed in me, who told me I could do it: *Nope. I came up short again.*

PART 1

# REJOICE, WE CONQUER

*"Way before we were scratching pictures on caves or beating rhythms on hollow trees, we were perfecting the art of combining our breath and mind and muscles into fluid self-propulsion over wild terrain. And when our ancestors finally did make their first cave paintings, what were the first designs? A downward slash, lightning bolts through the bottom and middle – behold, the Running Man."*

— CHRISTOPHER MCDOUGALL

# CHAPTER 1

What makes the Boston Marathon worthy of all this effort? Why are so many people like me determined to run it, particularly when there are countless other races to be conquered, the paths to them much easier and shorter, in some cases as simple as a click of the mouse? There are marathons large and small, quaint and legendary, flat and hilly – enough experiences to challenge, inspire and fulfill a runner for a lifetime, without ever traveling to Hopkinton, passing through Ashland and Framingham, climbing Heartbreak Hill, chasing down the famous Citgo sign and crossing the fabled finish line on Boylston Street.

You could try the fabulous New York City Marathon, for example. No other race in the world gives you the experience of crossing the Verrazano Narrows Bridge, traveling the five boroughs with two million spectators cheering you on, hitting the wall of sound on First Avenue and crossing the finish line in Central Park. I've done it three times and I'd go back in a New York minute.

There are plenty of other particularly well-organized events. I've finished the Walt Disney World Marathon, which takes you through Epcot, the Magic Kingdom and other Florida theme parks, and the Marine Corps Marathon, a tour of all of Washington's historic landmarks. Which organization – the U.S. Marines or Disney – has more control freaks who excel at logistics? It's too close to call.

And I have dozens of other races on my wish list. I'd love to run scenic Big Sur, the regal London Marathon, the flat course in Berlin where world records are routinely set. There are events known for their energy and emotion, like the Rock 'n' Roll Marathon in San Diego, and picturesque settings like Honolulu.

There are big races in Chicago and Philadelphia. There are well-regarded smaller marathons in Duluth and Pittsburgh.

If an urban race isn't interesting enough for you, you can run a marathon on the Great Wall of China or the frozen rock of Antarctica. There are even longer events, like the 56-mile Comrades Marathon in South Africa, the oldest ultramarathon in the world, and multi-day races like the Yukon Arctic Ultra.

And yet for me and for millions of other runners, no other event measures up to Boston. Ask someone to name the most prestigious marathon in the world, look at any comparison of the top destination races, and it's almost unanimous: Boston is at the top of the list.

What's so special about Boston? For one thing, it's the oldest marathon on the planet, launched in Victorian times, when McKinley was president, veterans of the U.S. Civil War still numbered in the tens of thousands and Thomas Edison had only recently founded his first electricity-generating station in New York City.

The Boston Marathon traces its roots back to the very earliest days of competitive long-distance running, almost thirty years before any other current marathon was created. It's unlikely that anyone who ran Boston in 1897 was still alive when the first New York City Marathon was staged seventy-three years later.

In more than a century of Boston Marathons, naturally, there have been dozens of historic moments. Johnny Kelley's heartbreak in 1936. Kathrine Switzer's daring entry in 1967. The legendary "duel in the sun" in 1982. Rick and Dick Hoyt's first of more than thirty races together in 1977. And, of course, the tragedy of the bombings on Boylston Street in 2013.

But there is more to Boston than just its vintage and its heritage. It is also exclusive. It is the race with a long lineup, not just a starting line but a guarded entrance. The gatekeeper is both fair and ruthless; only those who have earned their place are allowed to enter.

It is not about luck, apart from the benefit of good genes. A well-timed click in the first minute after registration opens will not get you to Hopkinton, nor will a providential entry in a lottery. You can enter through a very limited number of charity spots or travel packages, but the vast majority of participants receive a much-coveted invitation through the front door, making Boston the most elite, undemocratic and prized of all the marathons. By insisting on qualifying times, it is both cruel and inspiring, judgmental and alluring. Unlike any other race, a Boston entry is a validation of more than just a choice, but some combination of genetics and industry.

For a fortunate cohort of runners, Boston's qualifying times are well within reach. Some people qualify in their very first marathon. I am both deeply envious of and profoundly sympathetic to them. To win the lottery the day after signing your first mortgage is a stroke of good fortune that makes life instantly easier. No one would turn down the freedom. But those lucky souls are denied the value and satisfaction of a lifetime of working hard toward an ambitious goal.

For only the fastest runners is qualifying a routine accomplishment. To the rest, Boston remains a dream, resting tantalizingly on the spectrum somewhere between possible and impossible. Like many things in life that are just out of reach, it becomes an obsession. It's the oasis on the desert horizon, the chocolate éclair in the shop window.

Few runners think of qualifying in their first marathon. Typically, the only goal in a maiden voyage is to get to the finish line and find out if you have what it takes to cover the distance, regardless of how long it lasts. But after that, at some point early or late in a marathoner's career, a measurement is taken: how far am I from getting into Boston? How much older and how much faster must I become? What will it take to get there? You might try to put it out of your mind until you are of the right combination of age and speed to have a reasonable shot. But it doesn't help that you talk to dozens of people who have run Boston and rave about it. Sometimes they are wearing a brightly colored Boston

Marathon jacket when they do so.

And the more you hang around other runners, the more you get asked, "Have you run Boston?" and you have to explain that no, you haven't qualified yet, not even after six marathons, or a dozen, or more.

For many runners, then, it becomes an itch that must someday be scratched. You must attempt it, as the explorer George Mallory once said of climbing Mount Everest, because it is there. And so it becomes a question of when and how, not if. You cannot be satisfied until you've earned your place in Hopkinton and run to that famous finish line in Copley Square.

# CHAPTER 2

The marathon is ubiquitous today. There are races all over the world, covered live on television and profiled in human-interest stories. Even non-runners understand what a marathon represents, whether or not they can cite the precise distance. The meaning of the word has expanded to describe not just an organized long-distance footrace, but any extended or arduous task. *Marathon talks yielded no resolution to the teachers' strike. The dance marathon will raise money for the new gym equipment.* The expression "It's a marathon, not a sprint" is routinely applied to political campaigns, business ventures and other sustained endeavors.

But until 1896, Marathon was merely a town in Greece, the site of a famous battle 24 centuries earlier. In 1870, Marathon achieved brief international infamy as the place from which four English and Italian tourists were kidnapped and eventually murdered.

The profile of Marathon was changed permanently when, as most runners know, the organizers of the first modern Olympics were inspired by the legend of a Greek messenger. A man named Pheidippides, it was commonly believed, ran from Marathon to Athens, announced a glorious victory in battle by shouting "Nike!" – Greek for victory, not a reference to his trendy footwear – and then dropped dead from exhaustion.

Olympic organizers obviously saw more glory than tragedy in the fate of Pheidippides. They planned a race over the same route on the final day of the Games. Since then, the story of Pheidippides and the first Olympic marathon in his honor has become part of the lore of running. But the truth isn't so simple.

Did such a Greek messenger really exist? Was his name Pheidippides? Where did he actually run? And did he really expire at the finish line? There's almost as much debate about the story of

Pheidippides as the Kennedy assassination or Babe Ruth's called shot in the 1932 World Series. And, naturally, there is a lot less evidence to rely upon from the fifth century B.C. There are no closed-circuit tapes to review from that time, no electronic newspaper archives to browse. So how much of the story is true? How much is myth based on some loosely assembled facts? How much of it is pure fiction?

There's no doubt there was an epic Battle of Marathon in 490 B.C. When the smaller Athenian army fought off a Persian invasion about 26 miles from Athens, it was a turning point in European history. The victory strengthened the resolve of the Greeks, who won subsequent battles that protected their culture and set in motion two centuries of Classical Greek civilization. All that Greece gave the world – in politics and philosophy, scientific thought, theatre and literature – was preserved by the triumph on the plains of Marathon.

Naturally, much was written about this pivotal and unlikely victory. Herodotus, who established his place as the father of modern history by meticulously documenting politics and conflict in the Western Asia, Northern Africa and Greece of his time, wrote of Pheidippides in his masterpiece *The Histories*. Although it is considered the first history text of Western literature, the epic document was both factual and allegorical, and the story of the Athenian messenger was mostly the latter.

According to Herodotus, Pheidippides ran 150 miles without stopping, arriving in Sparta the day after he departed Athens, his mission to secure help from the Spartans in battle. He then ran back to Athens to complete his round trip. Along the way, if you accept this version of events, Pheidippides encountered the Greek god Pan, who offered to help the Athenians win the Battle of Marathon.

Apart from the bit about seeing Pan (which perhaps could be explained by a lack of proper hydration), the journey is not entirely far-fetched. Almost 2,500 years later, members of Britain's Royal Air Force attempted the trek themselves. Five men left Athens on October 8, 1982. Three of them arrived in Sparta less than 40 hours later. Every autumn since then, a Spartathlon race has been staged to replicate the feat. The course record, set in only the second race, is 20 hours and 25 minutes. This is no ordinary road race: according to the official Spartathlon website, the course travels through vineyards and olive groves, climbs steep hillsides – often in rainy, muddy conditions – and takes runners on a 3,500-foot ascent of Mount Parthenio, where Pheidippides saw Pan, in the dead of night. No assurances are given by race officials that Greek gods will appear to any modern runner.

How did Pheidippides' epic run transform from a two-day, 150-mile ultramarathon between Athens and Sparta to a mere 26-mile journey from Marathon to Athens? Some historians believe that his heroic journey was combined and confused with the return of the Athenians after their victory in Marathon. In the second century A.D., the Greek writer Lucian became the first to describe the now-familiar myth of Pheidippides having run from Marathon to announce the triumph, only to drop dead after delivering the news.

Lucian was a satirist, a Jon Stewart of his time, who scoffed at the serious writing of his contemporaries. So his version of events shouldn't have been taken at face value. Yet Lucian's account of Pheidippides somehow became the standard, replicated in the writings of Plutarch (although he gave the messenger a different name) and captured in sculpture and on canvas by two French artists centuries later. A nineteenth-century painting by Luc-Olivier Merson depicts an almost-naked Pheidippides in the prone position in front of Athenian leaders. There is no sign of any volunteers rushing to his side with a foil blanket and a bottle of water, or offering to take him to the medical tent. Perhaps they knew it was already too late.

All of this art and literature sustained the legend of Pheidippides but did little to popularize it; it was still largely an obscure piece of Greek mythology that stirred the creativity of only a handful of artists. But when Robert Browning was inspired to write about Pheidippides, everything changed. The British poet adapted the legend of the doomed Greek messenger into a compelling, 1,300-word piece broken into 15 stanzas, including this one:

So, when Persia was dust, all cried, "To Acropolis!
Run, Pheidippides, one race more! the meed is thy due!

Athens is saved, thank Pan, go shout!" He flung down his shield
Ran like fire once more: and the space 'twixt the fennel-field
And Athens was stubble again, a field which a fire runs through,
Till in he broke: "Rejoice, we conquer!" Like wine through clay,
Joy in his blood bursting his heart, he died – the bliss!

Whether or not he had ever experienced it himself, Browning captured the joy a runner feels when finally able to stop running after more than 26 miles. But while most marathoners relish the elation of a finish line, they prefer to escape the "bliss" of having their hearts actually burst.

Browning's tribute to Pheidippides likely would have been just another piece of art devoted to Greek history, if not for Michel Breal. A French semantics expert, Bréal was friends with Baron Pierre de Coubertin, who was then creating the modern Olympic movement. Bréal suggested that a 40-kilometer race be added to the first Games in Athens, as a way of adding a tough physical test and celebrating Greek history. De Coubertin liked the idea and placed the event on the final day of the Olympics, a tradition that lasts to this day.

Determined to see an athlete from the host nation win the special event, the Greeks ran a trial exactly one month before the Olympic marathon, a race that is believed to have been the first-ever marathon. The winner, Charilaos Vasilakos, finished in three hours and eighteen minutes. A few days before the Olympics, a second trial was organized. This time the winner was Ioannis Lavrentis, who finished in about three hours and eleven minutes.

A photo taken by Burton Holmes shows Greek runners training for the Olympics in 1896. It's not clear whether the picture was candid or staged, but it shows three men running in long pants along deserted roads.

At 2:00 in the afternoon on April 10, 1896, the first Olympic marathon was launched. A total of seventeen athletes started the race. Rather than rest for the endurance test, some of the runners had already competed in other distances in the same Olympics, including the 1,500-meter. Because of their unfamiliarity with the distance and perhaps due to fatigue from other events, seven men didn't finish.

As many as 100,000 people lined the roads and filled the stadium where the marathon would finish. Spiridon Louis of Greece won the race in just under three hours, capitalizing when the early frontrunners went too fast and eventually dropped out or even collapsed. He even had time to stop for a glass of wine in a village along the route, in what passed for an aid station in the nineteenth century. The win gave Louis the only gold medal for Greece at the Olympics and made him an instant national hero.

It also launched the marathon as the ultimate test of human endurance. It would take a long time before it became so popular that tens of thousands would attempt it at a time, in events around the world. But other similar races were soon being planned. And it was only a year later that another marathon was held in Boston.

# CHAPTER 3

Were it not for that epic finish to the first Olympic Games and the heroic efforts of a few New Englanders during the American Revolution, there would be no Boston Marathon on the third Monday of every April.

Only fourteen Americans competed at the 1896 Olympics, and the majority of them were from Boston. Several were students from Harvard University, but a few were members of the Boston Athletic Association.

In 1887, only nine years before the Olympics, the Boston Athletic Association had been founded with the goal of promoting "physical culture" and encouraging "all manly sports." The specifics about gender turned out to be a bit of unintentional foreshadowing of an event eighty years in the future, when a BAA official tried to tackle an unwelcome woman on the Boston Marathon race course.

The original BAA clubhouse was built on the corner of Exeter and Boylston Streets, on the site where the Boston Public Library's modern expansion is located today and only a few yards from the current finish line of the Boston Marathon. The club's facilities included a gymnasium, tennis courts, and a bowling alley. In 1890, the association launched its first track-and-field competition, a program which yielded some of America's first Olympians.

John Graham, a member of the BAA, was the manager of the first U.S. Olympic team. Tom Burke, a Boston University law student, won gold in the 100 meters and 400 meters in Athens. The two men were among those who watched the Olympic marathon on the final day of the Games, and they returned from Greece with the inspiration to launch a similar event in Boston.

In September of 1896, just a few months after the Olympic marathon, the Knickerbocker Athletic Club held its annual fall track-and-field competition. While other athletes competed in the usual events, about thirty long-distance runners took a train to Stamford, Connecticut and then ran back to the Columbia Oval in the first marathon held on American soil. The course was muddy, and even the leaders walked at several points on the course. The winner was John McDermott, in a time of three hours, twenty-five minutes and fifty-five seconds.

Only two years before the Olympics, the governor of Massachusetts, Frederic T. Greenhalge, had declared April 19 as Patriots' Day. Greenhalge was a native of Lancashire in the north of England who had moved with his parents to Lowell, Massachusetts when he was a teenager. He studied at Harvard, fought for the Union side in the Civil War, became a lawyer, and was eventually elected mayor of his adopted hometown.

The date was chosen in part to mark the anniversary of the Battles of Lexington and Concord, the first clashes of the American Revolutionary War, which occurred on April 19, 1775. On the night before the battle, Bostonian Paul Revere famously rode from town to town, warning of the approaching British army.

In other words, if Pheidippides had owned a horse or Paul Revere hadn't, then there probably wouldn't be a twenty-six-mile race every April in Boston.

Boston Athletic Association officials decided to hold the first American Marathon, as it was initially called, on Patriots' Day. In 1897 that happened to be on a Monday, but the tradition of Marathon Monday was more than seven decades away. Until 1969, Patriots' Day was always on April 19, no matter what day of the week that was. The marathon was always run on the holiday, unless it fell on a Sunday, in which case the race would be held on the Monday. In 1969, just months before Neil Armstrong walked on the moon, the holiday was fixed as the third Monday in April, and the marathon has been held on Monday ever since. So while most major marathons are held exclusively on Sunday mornings, the Boston Marathon has occurred on every day of the week except Sunday.

In 1897, Boston was approaching the end of a century of explosive growth. The city had struggled during the revolutionary war, as Britain first blockaded its port in response to the Boston Tea

Party and then laid siege to the city when they were driven back from Lexington and Concord by the revolutionary militia. The effects on Boston's economy and population were damaging. But during the 1800s, the city doubled in size roughly every twenty years.

With the end of the century approaching, Boston was bustling, one of the largest, busiest and most prosperous cities in America, with a population of half-a-million. The main downtown thoroughfare, Tremont Street, was routinely congested with a combination of pedestrians, horse-drawn carriages, trolleys and electric street cars. The solution, the first subway tunnel in North America, was almost finished. It wasn't quite the Big Dig that would dominate Boston headlines a century later, but the tunnel was a stunning example of modern infrastructure when it opened on September 1, 1897. In its first year of operation, it served fifty million passengers.

On the day of the very first Boston Marathon, cries of "play ball!" were heard, just as they are when the marathon is run today. But Fenway Park hadn't yet been built, and there was no Citgo sign for the runners to pass. On Patriots' Day in 1897, the Boston Beaneaters baseball club played their first game of the season, losing 1-0 to the Philadelphia Phillies. The Beaneaters struggled in April, earning only one victory in their first seven games. But, led by five future Hall of Famers, they went on to win ninety-three games and capture their fourth National League pennant of the decade.

The Beaneaters played at South End Grounds, about a mile to the southeast of where Fenway stands today. It would be another four years before the Boston Red Sox, now considered one of the oldest and most established teams in baseball, would begin playing in the newly formed American League.

The Red Sox and Fenway Park are just one of many modern-day sports and cultural institutions predated by the Boston Marathon. In 1897, the first World Series was still six years away. The Stanley Cup would not be awarded for another twenty. It would be another two decades before the National Football League was formed, another seventy years before the first Super Bowl. The game of basketball had only just been invented, and games still featured peach baskets from which men on ladders would retrieve the ball after points were scored – which wasn't very often.

William McKinley, the twenty-fifth American president and the last to have served in the Civil War, had just been sworn into office in March 1897 to preside over a union of forty-five states. Local prospectors had recently discovered gold in northern Canada, but the news had not yet reached America. When it did, in July 1897 in Seattle, it would spark the Klondike Gold Rush. Also that year, Mark Twain announced to a New York newspaper that "the report of my death was an exaggeration." The first patents for automobiles had only just been awarded. Orville and Wilbur Wright were still making bicycles.

There are few things about life in 1897, in Boston or anywhere else in North America, that are consistent with modern-day existence. But one thread stretches through the years, connecting the late nineteenth century to the present day. In April of 1897, the Boston Athletic Association launched a race that has been run, following almost entirely the same path, every single year since.

# CHAPTER 4

At 12:15 p.m. on April 19, 1897, Tom Burke scraped the heel of his boot across the narrow dirt road in front of Metcalf's Mill in Ashland, Massachusetts to create the starting line for the American Marathon, as the inaugural edition of the Boston Marathon was called. As a reporter described it at the time, Burke called for the contestants and fifteen men answered.

Burke was the son of a Boston undertaker and still in his early twenties. According to historian and author Patrick Kennedy, when Burke was growing up he was a tall, skinny kid who walked with a crutch because of rheumatism. Doctors feared the condition would be permanent, but as a teenager he won regional and then national 400-meter titles. He took six weeks off from his law studies at Boston University to travel by steamship to Greece, compete in the Olympics, and return home as the first 100-meter and 400-meter champion in modern history.

It's unlikely any of the fifteen men he beckoned to the makeshift starting line would have even heard of a marathon two years earlier. While they might have been eager to participate in a race, they didn't relish the long-distance journey to Boston quite the way tens of thousands covet it today. It's likely that most of them had little idea what they were in for, having never run even half as far in one stretch as they were about to on that spring day. There would have been no talk of fueling or hydrating, pace bunnies or split times.

According to a marvellous account in the next day's *Boston Globe*, the athletes ate in the dining room of a hotel just before the race, the competitors from New York at one table, those from Boston and Cambridge at another.

At 12:19 p.m., Burke started the race by simply shouting "Go!" The *Globe* reported that the contestants went away quickly, "but after going about 50 yards they seemed to realize they had just 25 miles of hard road before them and settled down to a comfortable jog." So new was this race to its readers that the *Globe* put the word "Marathon" in quotation marks.

The crowd in Ashland was strong and supportive: "The sleepy old town rang with the cheers of her lusty sons," the *Globe* wrote. Many of the spectators took the morning train from Boston to Ashland to see the start, then returned in time to witness the finish. They stretched in a line from Ashland to South Framingham, along with local residents who waved handkerchiefs from their doorsteps along the route.

Somewhere beyond Framingham, a convoy of bicycles, carriages, wagons, motorcycles – "in fact, every conceivable form of conveyance" – fell in behind the leaders. It was "as if the heavens had suddenly opened and rained wheels," the *Globe* said.

The course was designed to match the original route in Greece, a race back to downtown from almost twenty-five miles outside the city, over hills and dusty roads. The finish line would be in the Irvington Street oval, a 220-yard track that was the closest thing Boston had to the Olympic stadium in Greece.

The early lead was shared by Dick Grant, a Canadian student at Harvard, and Hamilton Gray of New York, with John McDermott of New York, the man who had won the marathon in his hometown the previous autumn, in third place. The runners continued to receive ovations along the route, to which they raised their hands or even bowed. The order didn't change much in the miles ahead, but on a hill between Wellesley and Newton Lower Falls, McDermott caught the leaders, then passed them on the downward slope.

"He evidently took the heart out of Gray, for he stopped running and walked," the *Globe* reported. It would be decades before the heartbreak that immortalized another hill in Newton. Grant continued to chase McDermott and the two raced each other for about a mile. Eventually, at the next big hill, Grant too stopped running, watching the New Yorker disappear around the next turn. Grant then beckoned the driver of a passing street-watering cart. "He laid down in the street, requesting the driver to let the water run over him." He tried to resume running but eventually gave up.

McDermott later described Grant as "the hardest man I ever beat. He held me for a mile, although he was all pumped out. If he had trained for the race he would have given me a hard race. As it was it was hard enough to shake him. He ran the pluckiest race I ever saw."

It took some effort to keep the road clear of spectators so McDermott could pass. The *Globe* reported he was running "like clockwork. His legs seemed to rise and fall like a phantom Greek and his little body was bent just the least bit forward, his arms were at full length at his side, and his face was set with determination." Apparently as McDermott ascended the next hill, he laughed at the cyclists who had a hard time keeping up with him. "He breasted the long hill manfully, still maintaining the beautiful form, and he laughed at the wheelmen who were pounding their pedals in their endeavor to keep their machines in motion."

But after twenty miles, McDermott started to experience a cramp in his leg. He stopped to rub the aching limb on more than one occasion, testing it out for a few hundred yards only to halt again. Some spectators thought that he, like Gray and Grant, would have to quit, but a combination of running and walking brought him closer to the finish, where he was advised that another runner was approaching. "He shut his teeth, set his face, and leaning well forward, he dug his shoes into the hard Beacon Street surface and started on his last spurt. He ran up the hill like a half-miler, down the other side to Commonwealth Avenue and across Massachusetts Avenue, breaking a funeral procession and stalling two electric cars."

At the Irvington Street oval, which stood just yards from the present-day Boston finish line, the cheers of the crowd were reported as deafening. "Every available foot of standing room in the oval was crowded," the *Globe* reported. "The policemen forgot their duty in the excitement, and the track was soon swarming with excited people, all wishing to grasp the hand of the victor of the first 'Marathon race' ever held in Massachusetts."

McDermott arrived on the track "with a bound" and circled it in exactly forty seconds to become the first Boston champion. He had now won the only two marathons ever raced on American soil. The *Globe* says he was lifted to the shoulders of the crowd. McDermott had finished in a time of two hours, fifty-five minutes and ten seconds. It was better than the winning time in Greece, so it was proclaimed as a world record. The first of many headlines in the *Globe* was "Record Time." But the courses were not exactly the same length and it was years before the marathon distance was standardized.

"Yes, I feel pretty tired in my legs," he told the reporter at the finish line. "My body is all right, but my feet are pretty sore, of course. My toes are blistered and the skin has peeled off the bottom of my feet."

McDermott was not a big man – the *Globe* called him the "little champion of champions" and the "little New Yorker" – but he claimed to have lost nine pounds in the race, from the one-hundred and twenty-three pounds he carried to the start. He went on to praise the route, saying it was "the best in the country. It is just uneven enough to make it interesting. It is a great deal better than the New York course." He added, "Everything connected with the race was managed a great deal better."

Then McDermott vowed he would never run another long-distance race. "I hate to quit now," he said, "because I will be called a quitter and a coward, but look at my feet. Do you blame me for wanting to stop it? I only walked about a quarter of a mile in the whole distance, and it was 20 miles before I lagged a step." He soon added, "I think I shall be all right tomorrow."

Like so many future marathoners, McDermott broke his finish line promise. He was back the following year to run Boston again.

Ten of the fifteen men who started the race finished the first Boston Marathon. The detailed and dramatic account in the newspaper was accompanied by a collection of illustrations under the headline "Incidents of the marathon road race." One picture portrayed spectators, including one woman, watching the runners lining up at the start. Another drawing showed "The Ambulance Corps," a handful of men on bicycles with crosses on their arms who, reports say, distributed lemons, water and wet handkerchiefs to the runners. A sketch labelled "A Stragler" showed a comically and profusely sweating runner next to a signpost for Boston. Finally, the winner was shown with his head held high as he strode confidently to the finish.

The "Marathon" race, the *Globe* reported, "proved a great success and is an assurance of an annual fixture of the same kind." Little did the newspaper know how prophetic was its prediction.

# CHAPTER 5

It turned out to be a good thing that Clarence DeMar didn't follow his doctor's advice. After being warned more than once that a heart murmur and long-distance running were a recipe for an early death, DeMar went on to become the most successful runner in Boston Marathon history and one of distance running's first and biggest stars.

DeMar was born in 1888 in Madeira, Ohio, a small town with a few dozen homes just to the northeast of Cincinnati. In 2007, BusinessWeek rated Madeira one of the best places in America to "raise kids for less." But in the late nineteenth century, the DeMar family had no choice but to get by on less. Clarence was born into poverty and hardship. His father died when he was ten years old; his mother moved the family to Massachusetts and put her son in a school for orphans.

Many years later, DeMar's son wrote in a letter to the Boston Athletic Association that his father hated the school so much that when he was asked about it, he flew into a "three-day rage." It was a "hard and somewhat squelched life," the elder DeMar said. But he performed well enough to earn a spot at the University of Vermont, where he chose to run cross country because he knew he didn't have any talent for football, baseball or boxing. After winning a ten-mile race, he decided to enter the 1910 Boston Marathon, where he finished second.

A physician who examined him later that year announced, "You have a bad heart." The doctor said he should give up running. "You shouldn't even walk upstairs."

DeMar demurred and was back at the starting line the following year. Before the marathon began, race doctors listened to his heart. According to one account, they told him, "You have a murmur. We must recommend that you drop out if you feel fatigued. And you really must stop running any more races." Less than two hours and twenty-two minutes later, DeMar crossed the finish line in first place, setting a course record.

It was an outcome he had foreseen. Just a few nights before the race, he wrote in his autobiography, "I dreamt distinctly that I had won the big race. Of course, I know such things are just a coincidence, but I was glad of the encouragement."

Not long after competing in the 1912 Olympic Marathon, DeMar did take a break from competitive racing for several years; his reasons included work, his studies at Harvard and Boston University and, to some extent, the nagging but unfounded concerns about his cardiovascular health.

DeMar did compete in the 1917 Boston Marathon without significant training. He had learned he would be going off to war and figured, "Why not have a little fun at marathoning first?" He finished third.

After World War I, he started training seriously again and became the most famous and prolific marathon runner of the Roaring Twenties. DeMar won Boston three straight times, in 1922, 1923 and 1924. He won a bronze medal in the 1924 Olympic marathon. He won races all over America. He regained the Boston title in 1927 and repeated as champion in 1928. His seventh and final Boston victory came in 1930, nineteen years after his first, when he was forty-one years old. No one else, man or woman, has won more than four times.

He became known as "DeMarvellous" and "Mr. DeMarathon." The *Globe* compared him to a Hollywood starlet: "His legs may not be as shapely as Claudette Colbert's, but they are equally famous." His status in running was so unrivalled that he titled his autobiography simply "Marathon."

But DeMar didn't like too much attention; while he had both a sense of humor and a sense of duty, he was notoriously stern and occasionally bad-tempered. He often accused spectators of distracting him. "Any word or deed aimed to get my attention would be like throwing a monkey wrench into a fine piece of machinery," he wrote. "Just a personal word like 'Step on it there' or 'Get going, Clarence' and I felt furious." Once a drunken spectator jumped onto the course to shake hands with him; DeMar punched him.

If he didn't like being watched or too loudly encouraged, he did love to run. DeMar didn't just train for events. He ran to work. He ran to Boston University, where he continued his education and eventually earned a master's degree. He ran everywhere, one of his friends once said.

Over almost fifty years, he entered races of virtually every possible distance, from one mile to forty-four. He finished almost one hundred marathons. According to the *Boston Globe*, he once ran and hitchhiked more than a hundred miles to participate in a ten-mile race, only to find out he had arrived a week early. So he ran and hitchhiked home.

When he was forty-nine, DeMar finished seventh at the Boston Marathon. When he was fifty-four, he still made the top twenty. In 1951, DeMar ran his one thousandth race, a ten miler on Columbus Day in Boston. His crotchety humor showed up in a quote in the *New York Times*: "It was a good race. It's the first race I can remember in which I was almost hit by only one car. These American motorists, you know, anything to save a minute."

He finished thirty-first out of forty-two men, at the age of sixty-three. "I just ran because I like to run," he told the *Times*. "I expect to continue running until I feel like stopping. And that's when I no longer get a kick out of it." DeMar ran Boston for the thirty-third and final time in 1954, when he was sixty-five. He finished in less than four hours.

Clarence DeMar died of stomach cancer in 1958, a few days after his seventieth birthday and a year after his final race, a fifteen-kilometer event in Maine. A few days later, his heart was examined by a renowned cardiologist named Dr. Paul Dudley White. White was an early advocate for the benefits of exercise to the cardiovascular system and was an avid walker and cyclist. He also served as President Dwight D. Eisenhower's physician and would later receive the Presidential Medal of Freedom from Lyndon Johnson.

According to the *New York Times*, White told students at Boston

University that the organ that had almost kept DeMar from running was actually in wonderful condition and had not been damaged at all by years of distance running.

The doctor who in 1910 had first suggested DeMar stop running died of heart disease less than a year after issuing his dire warning. According to the *Boston Globe*, DeMar was fond of saying, "I've always insisted that the physician had been listening to his own heart, not mine."

# CHAPTER 6

Clarence DeMar was one of many heroes of the first seven decades of the Boston Marathon, when the race drew significant attention but a small number of participants, at least in relation to modern marathons. In a time when everyday life was more laborious and running gear and training techniques were primitive, endurance running was largely an obscure sport populated by a small but committed community of amateur athletes.

Of the roughly 650,000 people who have crossed the finish line of the Boston Marathon in the past one-hundred and twenty years, more than 600,000 have done it since 1980. Prior to 1964, the race never had as many as even three hundred participants in one year. The fastest athletes raced for glory, not cash; there was no prize money until 1986.

Tom Longboat, an Onondaga runner from Ontario, was described as "the most marvelous runner who has ever sped over our roads" by the *Boston Globe* when he won the 1907 marathon. Canadians won seven of the first nineteen Boston Marathons, including three of the first five. Finishing third in 1907 was Johnny Hayes, who went on to win the 1908 Olympic marathon, touching off a period known as "marathon mania," when worldwide interest in the distance spiked and showdown events among the planet's best runners were regularly scheduled.

In 1917, there were calls for the Boston Marathon to be cancelled. Less than two weeks earlier, the United States had entered the Great War and there were fears that Boston Harbor might be under attack by German submarines that had recently sunk supply ships in nearby Atlantic waters. It was determined that the marathon should become a show of fitness and solidarity and so the race proceeded. New York bricklayer Bill Kennedy won in a showdown with two Finnish runners. In a display of American patriotism, Kennedy had said before the race, "We must repel the Finns." The *Globe* suggested the crowd was the largest at any marathon in history.

Along with Bricklayer Bill, among those early Boston champions were a mill weaver, a milkman, a plumber and a delivery boy. Many in the 1920s were military veterans. In 1925 Chuck Mellor of Chicago beat Clarence DeMar, running with a wad of tobacco in his cheek and having placed a copy of the *Boston Globe* under his shirt to protect him from the wind.

In 1934, Johnny Kelley, a florist's assistant from Arlington, Massachusetts, battled with a Finnish-born cobbler from Ontario named Dave Komonen. Kelley challenged Komonen for the lead several times until finally falling behind with five miles remaining. It was the first of a few disappointments for Kelley, including the one that was immortalized in the name of Heartbreak Hill.

But Kelley also became the most prolific and beloved runner in the history of the Boston Marathon. He won the race in 1935 and 1945, and finished second a record seven times. From 1934 to 1950, he placed in the top five fifteen times.

According to his obituary in the *Globe*, Kelley had wanted to be a baseball player. But when he was twelve years old, his father took him to watch the finish line of the marathon and he was hooked. For decades, he was synonymous with the race, so much so that "Here comes Johnny Kelley" became a familiar refrain sung by spectators along the route.

There's a monument to Kelley just to the side of the course in the Newton Hills, depicting both a younger and older version of the accomplished runner. It's not easily visible from the route on race day, buried in some trees and behind the spectators. But many runners make a separate trip to Newton to see the monument.

Kelley ended up running Boston sixty-one times, the last when he was eighty-four years old. "The Boston Marathon was his heart and soul," his nephew told reporters when Kelley died in 2004 at the age of ninety-seven.

Like so many Boston champions of his time, Kelley was an

amateur. He never collected any prize money and labored full-time in electrical maintenance, doing his marathon training in the evenings after a physically demanding day at work. He claimed that running offset the harsh conditions of his job, including working with asbestos.

"The fact that I ran at night after work, in the fresh air, probably saved my life," he said. "I owe an awful lot in this world to my running."

In another interview, Kelley said: "People always ask me why I keep on running. I keep running because I love it. To me, there's nothing else like it in the world."

# CHAPTER 7

At the 1928 Olympics in Amsterdam, the legendary Finn Paavo Nurmi won his ninth gold medal in the 10,000 meters. Johnny Weissmuller, the future movie Tarzan, won two gold medals in swimming. And several conventions were established that continue at the Olympics to this day: a flame was lit at the opening ceremonies, the athletes from Greece, the founding country of the modern games, marched first in the parade of athletes, and all the events were condensed into a sixteen-day schedule spanning three weekends.

But something happened at the 1928 Olympics that set back women's running for about half a century. For the first time, women competed in athletics. But according to several media reports at the time, the 800-meter race ended in disaster, with several women collapsing at the finish line.

"Below us on the cinder path were eleven wretched women, five of whom dropped out before the finish, while five collapsed after reaching the tape," wrote John Tunis of the *New York Evening Post.* Other journalists followed up by reporting that running was dangerous to a woman's reproductive system, or that it caused women to age prematurely.

Faced with such a distressing sight, Olympic officials withdrew the 800-meter women's race from future games. Hey, it was their duty to protect women from the potential for grievous and irreparable harm after two-and-a-half minutes of running, right? So until 1960, women were not allowed to move more than 200 meters at a time at the Olympics. The widespread belief, supported by purported experts who cited medical evidence, was that even medium-distance running was unhealthy for women.

To this day some people refer back to the collapsing women in 1928, even as they're deploring the resulting restrictions that were imposed on women for decades. But the media reports were no more factual than the legend of Pheidippides meeting Pan. According to running historian Roger Robinson, there were nine women in the race and all of them finished. One competitor fell after leaning across the finish line, but was helped to her feet after a few seconds. Others lay down to rest after a tough race. The film footage of the event shows no collapses.

Olympic organizers had been pressured into including a wide range of women's track and field events in the 1928 games. The all-male committee resisted and added only a handful of competitions, which led to a boycott of the women's events by the United Kingdom. So there was already a bias against women's participation, and all it took was a bit of erroneous media reporting to justify rolling back the clock and keeping women away from running anything but sprints for decades.

Today, there is evidence that women not only thrive in long-distance events, but might even be better-suited to them than men. In 2002, Pam Reed became the first woman to be the overall winner at the Badwater Ultramarathon. Billed as the world's toughest footrace, Badwater is a scorching test of one-hundred and thirty-five miles through Death Valley. In 2003, Paula Radcliffe set the women's world record at the London Marathon in a time that was less than ten minutes off the men's standard. In 1970, the gap between the men's and women's bests was more than fifty-three minutes.

Less than six months before Reed was born, the 800 meters was restored to the Olympics at the 1960 games in Rome. But that was it; women were not allowed to run more than half-a-mile. The limit remained in place for the 1964 and 1968 Olympics. Perhaps organizers needed to make sure that it wasn't just a fluke that the entire field hadn't collapsed at the finish line.

In 1972, a women's 1,500-meter race, just slightly less than a mile, was added. That was the limit for the next three Olympics, until finally, in 1984, women were allowed to run in a 3,000-meter race and the marathon.

That was twelve years after women were officially allowed to run the Boston Marathon, and eighteen years after they started doing so. The trail was blazed primarily by two women.

Bobbi Gibb says she fell in love with the Boston Marathon in 1964. "I was running through the woods with the neighborhood dogs when I first saw it," she once wrote. "I didn't know the marathon was closed to women."

Gibb started training seriously. Her boyfriend would drive her somewhere on his motorcycle and she would run home. She gradually increased her distance from one mile to ten. Eventually she was running back and forth to school, where she studied sculpture. She didn't follow a specific training program or book, and she ran in nurse's shoes because there was no footwear designed for female runners.

"For me, running was a form of communion with nature and a way to rejoin my mind and body," Gibb wrote.

Gibb and her dog Moot traveled across the United States in a Volkswagen bus in 1965. Every day, she says, she ran for hours in a new place – "the hills of Massachusetts, the grassy fields of the Midwest, the open prairies of Nebraska, the Rocky Mountains, the Sierra Nevadas, the coast of California. I'd never seen this earth before, and to me it was wondrous."

Some of her runs extended to forty miles, more than one-and-a-half marathons. "I'd see the top of a distant mountain, small and pale blue in the distance, and I'd spend all day running there, just to stand on the top. Then I'd turn around and run back. I made camp and slept outside every night, feeling infinitely close to nature. I was on a spiritual journey discovering something basic about existence."

After she moved to California, she kept running long distances. According to ESPN, one day, while running on a beach from San Diego, she accidentally ran into Mexico and was detained by border security officials when she returned to the U.S.

Gibb wrote a letter to the Boston Athletic Association, asking for an application to the 1966 marathon. The race director wrote back saying women were not physiologically capable of running a marathon distance. *All the more reason to run*, she thought. "At that moment, I knew that I was running for much more than my own personal challenge. I was running to change the way people think. There existed a false belief that was keeping half the world's population from experiencing all of life. And I believed that if everyone, man and woman, could find the peace and wholeness I found in running, the world would be a better, happier, healthier place."

Gibb's journey to the marathon, on a bus from San Diego to Boston, took three nights and four days. She arrived the day before the race. The following morning, Gibb's mother drove her to Hopkinton. Gibb hid in the bushes near the start and jumped into the pack after the gun went off.

Gibb has said that she was afraid she would be thrown out of the race, that the police might arrest her, that spectators might boo. She tried to disguise her appearance by wearing a hooded sweatshirt and her brother's shorts, but it wasn't long before other runners realized she was a woman. She says they were supportive and friendly. And after she took off her sweatshirt, so were the crowds.

By the time she reached Wellesley College, the women's university at roughly the halfway point of the course, the word had gotten out that a woman was running the Boston Marathon. Spectators were screaming and crying. "I felt as though I was setting them free," she wrote.

When she finished the race, the governor of Massachusetts shook her hand. The story was reported internationally. "It changed the way men thought about women, and it changed the way women thought about themselves," Gibb wrote. "It replaced an old false belief with a new reality."

Gibb ran again in 1967. This time, there was a woman registered for the race. But it wasn't her.

Like Bobbi Gibb, Kathrine Switzer had been told by someone that a woman couldn't complete a marathon. In 1967, when she was a journalism student at Syracuse University, she registered for Boston using her initials, K.V. Switzer, and received bib number 261.

On race day, Switzer says, she didn't try to disguise her appearance. Because of the weather, she was wearing a sweatshirt and sweatpants.

But her hair wasn't hidden and she says she was wearing makeup. What followed has been documented many times. A couple of miles into the marathon, a race official named Jock Semple discovered Switzer and tried to physically remove her from the course. Switzer says he screamed, "Get the hell out of my race and give me those numbers."

Jock Semple was born in the slums of Glasgow in 1903. According to the Scottish newspaper the *Daily Record and Sunday Mail*, he lived "in a crumbling, cold one-bedroom apartment" with his parents and two brothers and learned from a young age to "punch first and talk later." Semple moved to the U.S. in 1921 and worked as a cabinetmaker in Philadelphia. After running the Boston Marathon, he moved to Massachusetts and began working in sports, as a trainer for Olympic athletes and a physical therapist for the Bruins and Celtics.

Eventually, he became the co-director of the Boston Marathon, a role he carried out very earnestly. An article in *Sports Illustrated* describes how Semple would physically and verbally attack anyone who didn't seem to be taking the race seriously. He called them weirdos and screwballs. One year he tackled a runner wearing swimming fins and a snorkeling mask.

To Semple, Kathrine Switzer was not welcome in the Boston Marathon because she was breaking the rules. Women were not just discouraged from running Boston, they were banned from the marathon and other long-distance races by the Amateur Athletics Union.

Switzer was running alongside her boyfriend, an athlete named Tom Miller. After Semple grabbed Switzer's sweatshirt, Miller knocked him out of the way. The incident was captured in photographs that were soon shared around the world and, eventually, in a Time-Life book called *100 Photos that Changed the World*.

Switzer finished the race, crossing about an hour after Gibb, who had once again participated as a non-registered runner. But she wasn't welcomed or congratulated at the finish line. She was disqualified from the event and expelled from the Amateur Athletics Union.

Switzer became an advocate for women's running, won the New

York City Marathon in 1974, launched a global running series for women, and wrote a book.

Semple is known for his attempt to physically remove Switzer from the course. But he was also a pioneer who was instrumental in changing the rules he once enforced. In 1972, he and other race officials opened the race to women. At the start line of the 1973 Boston Marathon, Semple and Switzer reconciled. A photo of them embracing appeared in the *New York Times* the following day. The two were friends for the next fifteen years until Semple died in 1988.

Bobbi Gibb was honored as the grand marshal of the 2016 Boston Marathon, fifty years after she was the first woman to cross the finish line.

In 1972, eight women registered and ran the Boston Marathon. None of them collapsed at the finish line.

# CHAPTER 8

When you first glance at a picture of Bill Rodgers from the 1975 Boston Marathon, you might think he was an eccentric local runner hoping simply to finish, not an elite athlete competing for the podium. He's wearing a t-shirt – legend says he pulled it out of a trash can – on which he has written with a felt-tip pen "Boston GBTC." His bib number 14 is attached at a bit of an angle. He has on painter's gloves that his brother bought for him from a hardware store in Hopkinton because his hands were cold. He's sporting a headband that makes him look a bit like Wimbledon champion Bjorn Borg. He's running in brand-new shoes – a cardinal sin among modern marathon runners – that were sent to him by Steve Prefontaine, samples from a relatively unknown shoe company called Nike. He's not even wearing a watch.

Rodgers was a graduate student at Boston College and ran with the Greater Boston Track Club – that's what the GBTC on his shirt represented. He failed to finish the 1973 Boston Marathon, dropping out on Heartbreak Hill. In frustration, he quit running for three months. In 1974, he ran Boston again and placed a respectable fourteenth in just over two hours and nineteen minutes. He won that fall's Philadelphia Marathon, but in an even slower time.

No one thought of him as a future Boston champion. But a few weeks before the 1975 race, he captured a bronze medal at the world cross-country championships in Morocco. Rodgers later told *Runner's World* that he felt "I can run with anyone now."

Rodgers was also driven by a sense of local pride, saying he wanted the race to belong to a Bostonian. Eight miles into the marathon, he was racing side-by-side with Canadian Jerome Drayton.

"I remember someone yelling, 'Go Canada!'" Rodgers told *Runner's World* forty years later. "It really got me fired up, and I surged and I made my move. I think Jerome didn't know who the heck I was, and he let me go."

He ran the rest of the course alone. At the bottom of Heartbreak Hill, he stopped to tie his shoe. In the final few miles, he stopped four more times to drink water. Rodgers says he simply found it easier to gulp down fluids while he was standing still.

As he approached the finish, Rodgers was told by race official Jock Semple that he was going to break the course record. Rodgers says he was shocked. He finished in just under two hours and ten minutes, knocking almost ten minutes off his previous best time.

The 1975 race was historic for another reason. Bob Hall completed the course in a wheelchair, finishing in just under three hours. The milestone led to the creation of a wheelchair division.

Rodgers' victory launched him into the upper echelon of distance runners. Over the next six years, he won sixteen of the twenty-five marathons he entered. He won New York four times in a row, from 1976 to 1979. He won Boston three more times, from 1978 to 1980. In 1978, he won twenty-seven of thirty races he entered.

Boston Billy became an endearing icon of endurance sports, an Olympian and record-breaker who had more in common with the everyday runner than the typical elite athlete. He talked often of his love of cheeseburgers. One of his victories in New York was run in a pair of newly acquired soccer shorts, because he forgot to pack his shorts for the race. He made marathon running seem more accessible and he inspired a generation of amateur runners, launching the first running boom.

Rodgers continued to run long after his competitive days were over. In 1996, he ran a sub-three-hour Boston at the age of 48. In 1999, he fell victim to dehydration and had to pull out. He was determined that would not be his last marathon. He joked to the *Wall Street Journal* in 2002, "I can't have my last marathon in Boston be a DNF (did not finish). This is unacceptable."

In 2009, sixty-one years old and having survived prostate cancer, Bill Rodgers ran Boston again and finished in just over four hours.

When Rodgers won his fourth Boston Marathon in 1980, he raised four fingers as he crossed the finish line. The historic win put him in exclusive company. Other than Clarence DeMar, only Gerard Côté of Canada had won four times (Robert Kipkoech Cheruiyot of Kenya later joined the group with his fourth win in 2008). But despite the historic occasion, it was the women's race that brought the marathon international attention and infamy that year.

Rosie Ruiz was born in Cuba and moved to Florida as a child, then New York City. In 1979, she was the eleventh woman to cross the finish line at the New York City Marathon, earning a trip to Boston. On April 21, 1980, she appeared to win the Boston Marathon in 2:31:56, twenty-five minutes faster than her time in New York and four minutes faster than any woman in Boston history. Very quickly, suspicions were raised. She didn't have a lot of knowledge about marathon training. She didn't appear to have the same physique as other elite athletes. And many runners and spectators said they didn't see her on various parts of the course.

Soon, witnesses came forward to say they had seen her enter the course half a mile from the finish. Another story emerged that she had traveled on the subway during the New York City Marathon. New York officials soon nullified her result from that race, which meant she had no longer qualified to run the marathon in Boston that she had supposedly won. Boston organizers did their own investigation and found no photo or television evidence of her at key points on the course. They soon disqualified her as well.

Just a few years earlier, Jacqueline Gareau had been working at a Montreal hospital when she joined a group of co-workers who had taken up running. She enjoyed it so much she kept running longer and farther. "I just kept running because running felt good to me," she said recently. "I loved running long distances."

She finished second in the Ottawa Marathon in 1978, then won the race the next year. In 1980, she planned to run Ottawa again, but a friend suggested she run Boston instead. It was a historic conversation for two reasons. The friend ended up becoming her husband. And Gareau ended up winning the Boston Marathon under unique circumstances.

Gareau thought she had finished second to Rosie Ruiz in Boston, and had returned to Montreal. A few days after the race, she was flown back down to Boston, where race officials set up a finish line with thousands of spectators so they could photograph her breaking the tape and present her with the medal. While she was denied the experience of winning on race day, Gareau assumed a special place among Boston champions. She has returned to Boston to a hero's welcome on milestone anniversaries of her 1980 victory. Ruiz, meanwhile, has continued to claim she ran the entire course.

In 1982, two Americans battled each other for twenty-six miles in what became known as the "duel in the sun." An entire book has been written about that race, featuring two very different but equally appealing stars: Cuban-American Alberto Salazar, who was the favorite and considered almost unbeatable at marathon distance, and Dick Beardsley, the challenger from rural Minnesota whose father had given him an IOU for a plane ticket to Boston as a high school graduation present and who had trained specifically for Boston by running Heartbreak Hill repeatedly, even in a blizzard.

A lot less was known about training methods in the early 1980s. Beardsley used to pound his thighs hundreds of times a day, thinking it was good for his muscles. Salazar ran extraordinary mileage in training, sometimes as much as two hundred miles in one week.

The two runners set a blistering pace and then battled together for the final nine miles. They were so close together that at one point when he was slightly ahead, Beardsley tracked Salazar by watching his shadow on the pavement. Both men described later how much they were hurting in the final five miles – Beardsley said he could no longer feel his legs and kept telling himself "one more mile." But each runner remained determined not to surrender.

With less than a mile to go, Beardsley's hamstring suffered and Salazar surged ahead. But somehow Beardsley managed to pour it on in the final few hundred yards and closed some of the gap. Both runners beat the previous course record, with Salazar winning by two seconds. Salazar was rushed to hospital and given six liters of fluid; despite temperatures in the seventies, he'd had barely anything to drink during the race.

The marathon was declared the greatest in Boston history; there were two winners that day, many observers proclaimed. Many thought it would be the start of a rivalry but the race took its toll on both athletes and neither matched that performance in the future. Salazar's decline was gradual. He won other races, including his third straight New York City Marathon that fall. But he noticed it took longer to recover from workouts and that he was always getting sick. This was no ordinary fall; Salazar was still only in his mid-twenties. A few years later, Beardsley suffered a horrifying accident on his farm. During his treatment he became addicted to painkillers. Now sober, he speaks as often to addicts as he does to runners.

In 1983, Joan Benoit won her second Boston Marathon. The day before the race, Norway's Grete Waitz broke Benoit's world record in winning the London Marathon. Benoit reclaimed the record, beating Waitz's time by more than two-and-a-half minutes. The two met the following year in the first-ever Olympic women's marathon. Once again, Benoit prevailed, by a minute, over Waitz.

The Boston Marathon has always had an international flavor. From 1946 to 1954, there were winners representing seven different countries. But until 1988, no one from Africa had ever won the race. When Ibrahim Hussein of Kenya won his first of three Boston championships that year, it touched off a remarkable period of dominance for runners from the Great Rift Valley. In the twenty-nine editions from 1988 through 2016, twenty-six of the men's winners have come from either Kenya or Ethiopia.

One of them, Kenya's Geoffrey Mutai, ran the fastest marathon ever in 2011, finishing in 2:03:02. It didn't count as a world record because Boston is a point-to-point course with a net loss in elevation. But it was a remarkable performance on what is often described as a tough course.

African women began their supremacy in Boston in 1997, when Fatuma Roba of Ethiopia won her first of three in a row. After that, Catherine Ndereba of Kenya won four times in five years. From 1997 through 2016, only two runners from Russia interrupted the streak.

Born in 1975 in Eritrea, Meb Keflezighi and his family were refugees who arrived in the United States when he was twelve years old. Keflezighi became a high school and university middle-distance champion. He won a silver medal in the 2004 Olympic marathon, the first American to win a medal since 1976. He won the New York City Marathon in 2009, the first American champion since 1982.

And on April 21, 2014, Meb Keflezighi not only won a race but captured the damaged hearts of thousands of runners and spectators.

PART 2

# A CHARISMATIC EVENT

*"Running is perhaps the most fundamental of all sports, and it is economically the least costly to perform. As a consequence, it is the most democratic and most competitive of all sports because individual merit can prevail despite economic inequality. It is a sport for everyone, the whole world over."*

**BERND HEINRICH**

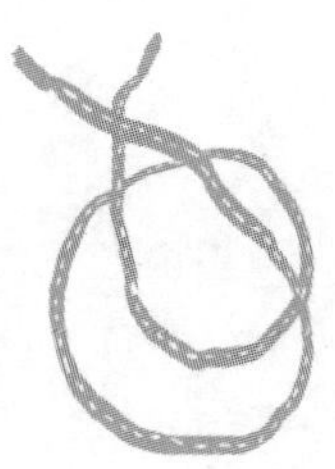

# CHAPTER 9

It's easy for many of us to remember where we were on April 15, 2013. Thousands, of course, were in Boston, before, at or beyond the finish line, caught completely off guard by the noise, the reaction, the bedlam. Others were watching from a distance as the events played out live on television, wondering what had caused the chaos and what it represented. And still more were caught off guard when they learned what had happened, from a friend or a news bulletin.

It's tempting to describe the attack as unimaginable, but no matter how shocking it was, it wasn't entirely unforeseen. A marathon route is almost impossible to fully secure, unless you want to dramatically alter the experience or substantially reduce the presence of spectators. A few years earlier at the New York City Marathon, I had shuddered at the thought of safeguarding a start line with more than 40,000 participants, organizers and volunteers, a finish line with four or five runners crossing every second, and, in between, a 26-mile playing field surrounded by two million spectators.

Whether it was in the front of our minds or not, marathons have always been a potential trouble target, and organizers and law enforcement officials at hundreds of events quietly consider the possibility of many different disaster scenarios, including terrorism. Unlike other major sports events, like the Super Bowl, that draw thousands of spectators but are held in much more secure environments, marathons are run in highly fluid conditions, on public streets with spectators and runners coming and going at all times. You don't need a ticket to watch a marathon, nor do you pass through a turnstile. To secure a marathon route fully is like trying to lock down a highway or a forest.

After the shock and beyond my concern for the victims, my first reaction was to wonder how inexorably marathon running had been changed by this single act. Would Boston and other races be forever different? How much would the structure of future events have to change? Would runners be deterred by the threat of violence? Would fewer spectators turn out? Even if marathoners still signed up for events, would they be less likely to bring their families along?

Or, perhaps worst of all, would the Boston Marathon be forever linked to this cowardly act of terror? Would the marathon, once a largely unblemished symbol of personal achievement and philanthropy, now be tainted with images of violence and risk? Would we allow this act of barbarism to overshadow the tens of thousands of moments of courage, charity and goodwill that play out at races every year?

In the early minutes after the attack, and perhaps for even longer than that, it was hard for runners not to take the whole thing personally. That final stretch on Boylston Street, after all, is the most coveted three-eighths of a mile in the world. For runners, it is the summit of Everest. Making those final few hundred strides to the cheers of thousands of Boston spectators is, for many of us, the achievement of a lifetime.

But was this a strategic target? Was the most famous marathon in the world chosen as a vehicle to make a specific statement? To be sure, the Boston Marathon could be considered a highly symbolic target. It's a gathering of thousands of people from all over the world, an unparalleled celebration of the human spirit. And on Patriots' Day, no less. Can there be any better emblem of freedom and camaraderie than a race with 24,000 participants of all ages, races and religions, running of their own free will, striving to achieve their dreams, with the flags of dozens of their countries lining the final few hundred yards?

Was the marathon, or what it represents, singled out for this attack? Or was it just that the event was the closest and most expedient target, a high-profile occasion at which a lot of people had gathered? It's impossible to know, but I doubt the perpetrators put as much thought into the symbolism of a marathon as so many of us have since it happened.

At the time, I worried that it would be a long time before our marathons were as carefree as before, when the only worry for runners was how well they would perform. Boston and so many other races, I assumed, would be forever altered.

In most respects, I was wrong. Some things have changed: the security at races, particularly Boston, has intensified. The process of checking a bag is much more cumbersome; in some cases, checked bags have been eliminated completely. But otherwise, almost every part of running a big-city marathon has returned to the way it was before. We didn't stop running. We didn't stop entering races. And we certainly didn't stop trying to get into Boston. Within days, thousands of Boston participants past and present were talking about going back the next year, to be part of the first marathon after the bombings, to show strength and solidarity. The race was in greater demand than ever before.

After a few marathons were run with increased security, and following a somber and respectful tribute to the victims one year later at the 2014 marathon, it didn't take long before we were once again thinking less about the threat of violence and more about the marathon as a symbol of hard work and persistence, the fulfillment of dreams. That doesn't mean we've forgotten what happened. But it does mean we won't let it stop us from running a good race, from sharing and enjoying the experience. We won't let marathons or running or anything else about our freedom be changed by a violent act. Some people have said Boston reclaimed the marathon in 2014, but I don't think it ever surrendered it in the first place.

The demonstrations of resilience, in Boston and elsewhere, have been overwhelming. The Boston Marathon has become more than a series of personal triumphs. It is now a demonstration of collective determination. The support for the victims and their families has been extraordinary. Some of their stories of recovery, a few of which have led them to the start line of the marathon themselves, are powerfully moving.

We will continue to create such stories, year after year, overshadowing the demons of 2013. These acts of free will and determination will help to diminish the perpetrators and their actions by giving them less and less importance with every passing moment. There is too much good in the world, and at the Boston Marathon, for two men to eclipse with one dreadful attack.

The message has been sent, over and over again. We will not be deterred. Our freedom – to live and to run – will not succumb to fear. We will proclaim Boston Strong, and print it on our t-shirts, for years to come. But ultimately, the best way to respond to terrorists is not just to outshout them but to make them irrelevant. Even on that day, we must be reminded, while there were two people causing harm, there were tens of thousands doing quite the opposite: honoring hard work and achievement, supporting each other, raising millions of dollars for charities, celebrating life and humanity.

And in 2014, there was a special treat for the Patriots' Day crowds. Meb Keflezighi became the first American man since 1983 to win the Boston Marathon. Keflezighi's execution was flawless, his timing sublime. The victory "gave Boston and America the victory the whole country longed for, but scarcely dared hope for, in the most emotional and significant of all 118 Boston Marathons," *Runner's World* wrote. "He did it with a courage and determination that the whole nation can be proud of. Boston today was a field of dreams."

# CHAPTER 10

When we think back to the events of 2013, it's important to remember that runners were neither the targets nor the victims of the bombs.

The explosives weren't placed on the course, but on the sidelines. As one runner said to me that week, the people who were hurt and killed were those who had been cheering runners on for the entire day. They didn't get the satisfaction of finishing a marathon. They weren't experiencing the culmination of a dream. They were just there to support those who were.

Indeed, while 24,000 athletes entered the race, only a few dozen were in the vicinity of each of the bombs when they went off. On a marathon course, runners are spread out over twenty-six miles. And they are constantly moving, never staying in one place for long. By the time the explosions occurred, many were already back in their hotel rooms. But there were thousands of spectators in close proximity to the finish line, many of whom hadn't moved in hours.

Collectively, those spectators are crucial to a marathon. We wouldn't want to do it without them. How many of us dream of crossing a finish line surrounded by silence? We've all run through quiet sections of other races and know how much less appealing and energizing it is. If it weren't for the spectators, a marathon wouldn't be much different from a long training run. It might be personally satisfying but it wouldn't be special, joyful, exhilarating.

Individually, almost every one of the spectators is important to someone on the course. They are our friends and family members, the saints who have indulged our dreams, put up with our training and come to the finish line to do nothing but witness, encourage and acknowledge our accomplishments. We don't just want the finish-line moment, the medal, the photo. We want the people closest to us to share it with us. We want them to chase us all over the course, if possible. We want them to see us cross the line. In this respect we are like children imploring "Look at me!" while they do a cartwheel for the first time.

Unlike at other sporting events, marathon spectators aren't paying fans who are there to watch a competition between people they've never met. A few might have some interest in the elite athletes, but most are there to see the ordinary runners. That's why there are so many signs talking about moms and dads, about husbands and wives and close friends, exhorting them to go faster, to dig deeper. No matter how quickly it happens, that brief moment of recognition can be electrifying for a runner. Those few seconds of hearing a familiar voice, seeing a friendly face, can be energizing and touching. Watching the events unfold from home, I couldn't help imagining, over and over again, my wife and kids waiting for me at that perilous finish line.

What do people talk about when they say the experience at a race was amazing? It's invariably the crowds. Even though each spectator is there specifically for one or two participants, most of them will cheer on all of us, totally unknown to them, for hours at a time.

So while many runners talked defiantly about not being deterred by the violence, about returning to Boston the following year, about running stronger, it wasn't really about us. If a bomb went off in the bleachers at Fenway Park, no one would be saying the Red Sox players shouldn't be deterred from playing again.

We should have been more concerned about whether the crowds would come back than whether the runners would. And they did return, in greater numbers than before. Their determination and resilience is as much a source of inspiration and is every bit as deserving of respect as the resolve of any runner – perhaps even more so, given that they have less to gain from the experience.

All of us should make more of an effort to show our appreciation for the people who were most at risk in Boston: the friends, family members and complete strangers who treat us like heroes and make the race experience unforgettable. Spectators are the soundtrack to our biggest dreams and our most cherished memories. Without them, not just race day but every day would be empty.

# CHAPTER 11

We might be confused into thinking that like so many other contests, the history of a marathon, especially one with the prestige and history of Boston, is told exclusively through the stories of its winners: the epic battles for the podium, the repeat champions, the course records and milestone achievements. The Boston Marathon, after all, is one of the world's premier sporting events, contested annually by the fastest distance runners on the planet, including world record holders and Olympic champions. The race is one of six included in the international major series. The winning man and woman in 2016 each received $150,000.

But the modern marathon is unique among world-class athletic competitions. There aren't thousands of nags who trundle behind the thoroughbreds during the Kentucky Derby. You can't enter the Tour de France as an amateur cyclist and pedal your way up and down the French Alps at half the speed of the elites. Nor can you drive your car onto the course of the Daytona 500 and pass under the checkered flag hours after the winner.

On the final day of the Masters, only five dozen golfers are allowed to swing their clubs. On the day the Wimbledon championship is awarded, only two athletes compete. But even at the Boston Marathon, with its stringent qualifying standards, some 30,000 runners participate, less than half of one percent of whom have even the slightest chance of winning. Of the 27,488 runners who started the 2016 Boston Marathon, only thirty-six finished within fifteen minutes of the champion of their gender category.

At most sports events, barriers are constructed between gods and mortals. The best play and the rest buy tickets. But at most marathons, the ordinary are invited to join the extraordinary. The field is opened to all. Don't just watch; come run with the best in the world.

A marathon, therefore, is so much more than a race. When the community of runners exploded in the 1960s and 1970s, it became an exercise in populism. Hundreds, then thousands, joined marathons not to compete but to complete, not to win but just to be in. Their stories are often just as inspiring as – if not more so than – those of the stars at the front of the pack.

More than an elite competition, the marathon has become a personal test, the proving ground of the ordinary. It is a chance both to discover and to define who you are. At some point in every marathon, you are asked a question. How you respond can alter the way you think of yourself. For many, it is nothing short of a life-changing event.

It begins with the fact that running is hard. There is barely anything that powers you other than your own energy and willpower. There are no wheels. It's not about the bike because there is no bike. You can't build up a bit of momentum and then coast.

And it's never harder than the first few times you do it. That first threshold is one of the greatest. When I set off with the goal of completing a three-mile run in roughly 30 minutes, my body ached after a hundred yards. My lungs were screaming. My legs were sending sharply worded telegrams to my brain demanding that I stop.

To get from there to a marathon is achievable for most humans, but only through deep commitment to a protracted journey of incremental gains. You can probably run a marathon, but you can't prepare for it in a day or a week or even a month. It takes time. Training for a marathon is like showing up at the office every day. It's Cal Ripken's streak. It's like putting aside small amounts for your retirement and watching them add up over the years. It's a two-thousand-piece jigsaw puzzle with many pieces of the same color. It's not a lottery ticket or a Cinderella story on *American Idol*. The moment is not thrust upon us. It is one we choose, many months in advance.

For some, a shorter distance like a 10k or a half-marathon can create a similar feeling of affirmation and empowerment. But the marathon is in a different category altogether. For most humans, both the distance and the time are on the far side of a line between practical and extreme. While we may be born to run, a marathon is not within our natural grasp. We weren't designed to run for three or four hours, nor to race from one town to the next (look what happened to Pheidippides).

As daunting as it is, however, the marathon is available to almost everyone. It seems like the pinnacle of personal achievement, and yet it is within reach. The marathon is both wildly ambitious and enormously democratic.

For the elite athlete from Africa, long-distance running is a coveted professional sport, the equivalent of a career in basketball or football for a North American kid. The economics are overwhelming: a win at one major event can feed a huge family back home for years. Some Kenyans have invested their winnings in cows and other farming assets and set themselves up for life.

For the amateur runner in the First World, however, it's a personal task, a proving ground. And what great lessons there are in going from nowhere to somewhere, even if it takes months or years. Perhaps especially if it takes months or years. Preparing for a marathon is like many other aspects of everyday life: work, marriage, parenthood. There are occasional moments of instant gratification but the greatest reward comes far down the well-traveled road.

"The marathon is a charismatic event," said Fred Lebow, the co-founder of the New York City Marathon. "It has everything. It has drama. It has competition. It has camaraderie. It has heroism. Every jogger can't dream of being an Olympic champion, but he can dream of finishing a marathon."

One of the reasons we seek out such physical challenges is that we are built for them. If we are hammers, then these are our nails. Most of us in the First World live better than the royalty of two hundred years ago, yet we are still hardwired for sacrifice and suffering, for the great demands our ancestors endured.

It doesn't even matter if we're not particularly good at running. Indeed, it may even be better that way. The less naturally you take to running, the more unlikely an athlete you are, the greater the challenge becomes and the more significant the achievement.

And we improve not only our running performance when we train. We afflict ourselves in our comfort and we learn, adapt and improve. It's not just our legs that are getting stronger with each run. As my friend, the adventure runner Ray Zahab, says, running is a great teacher. While you absorb hard data and anecdotal evidence about training methods, about lactic acid and slow-twitch muscles, about nutrition and hydration, about speed work and hills, it's not about kinesiology that you learn the most. You etch one of life's greatest lessons – that many great things are achievable if you approach them one step at a time – deep into your psyche. You learn a bit about the sport; you discover a great deal about yourself.

In its modern form, the marathon has become the domain of those who have overcome. The survivors of cancer and other scourges. The people living with disabilities. The war veterans. The recovering addicts. The mentally ill. It is the territory of unlikely heroes. The fundraisers. The moms of newborns. The refugees from lethargy, obesity and unhealthy behavior.

It can represent closure, a new beginning, proof of recovery. It can serve as a memorial, a tribute. It can simply be a statement about taking ownership of a small part of your life, acting instead of reacting.

For more than a decade, I've been drawn to the story of the ordinary runner. I've interviewed more than 2,500 runners for magazine and newspaper columns, books, and a weekly radio show and podcast. The mother who runs in memory of a lost child, raising money for research. The man who recovers from leukemia, then runs a marathon to prove he has conquered the disease. The sexual abuse survivor who has battled depression and addiction and for whom running is a healthy compulsion. The list and the sources of inspiration are endless.

Since 2013, there has been a new category of survivors who have run Boston. The spectators who lost limbs in the bombing, then decided to run the marathon a year or two later. The victims of post-traumatic stress disorder. The first responders who saved lives and treated the wounded, then came back to run the marathon the following year.

But even those whose stories aren't so dramatic are equally inspiring because they have found the drive to do something hard. There are thousands of individual stories, each of them uniquely rousing. And there is also something heroic and stirring about the entirety of it all, the collectivity of striving souls traveling the road together in a giant mass. In a marathon, just as in the human race, both the individuals and the multitudes matter.

# CHAPTER 12

In 1999, *New York Times* columnist and author Thomas Friedman proposed the Golden Arches Theory of Conflict Prevention. He argued that no two countries with McDonald's franchises had ever gone to war against each other.

It may not apply universally – whether or not they constitute war, there have been definite instances of conflict between countries with McDonald's restaurants. But Friedman's broader point is worth noting: that the same factors that tend to make a country suitable for an international fast-food chain – a certain level of prosperity and a large middle class – also make it less likely to be involved in international conflict with each other.

I think a similar argument could be made about countries that have a significant population of runners and at least one successful marathon. In order to have a race with thousands of participants, you must reach a certain level of economic success – otherwise people will be too focused on their day-to-day survival to have the energy or the penchant to pursue a long-term goal like training for a big race.

In the places where thousands of people train, running is very democratic. Long-distance races are great equalizers. They aren't class-conscious. At 10k events, half-marathons, and marathons all over the world, everyone lines up in the same corrals, with very little to distinguish the rich from the poor, the professional from the laborer, the North American from the African, the Catholic from the Jew.

I once trained for a half-marathon with a large group of runners. We were together every week for hours at a time, but I didn't find out many of their surnames until after the race. We had talked for hours about family, about developments in the news and, of course, about running. But in most cases we had never told each other what we did for a living.

Races are run in every nation on earth. But apart from schoolyard sprints for children, in many places competitions are staged only for elite athletes, many of whom are hoping running will be their ticket out of poverty and perhaps out of the country. For a long-distance race to be filled with thousands of ordinary adults, the local economy has to be sufficiently advanced that people can engage in physical activity as a pastime rather than an occupation. If citizens are preparing for a half-marathon or marathon in their spare time, their day-to-day existence must be secure and not so physically taxing that they are too exhausted to train. In developing countries, it would be unthinkable for many people to start or finish a day filled with exhausting manual labor by going for a run.

The most significant indicator of a country's advancement, though, is a marathon with a lot of female participants. A community has to be both safe and progressive for women to train for a long-distance race. How many places in the world are too dangerous for a woman to run alone? Is there any better indicator of the safety and equality of a society than to see a woman running by herself on a sidewalk or recreational path?

It's still an astonishingly recent phenomenon. I'm sure a lot of millennials would be shocked to hear that as recently as the 1960s, before Bobbi Gibb and Kathrine Switzer, it was considered unsafe for women to run more than a few hundred yards. We've come a long way since then. In our society, men and women run side-by-side and in almost equal numbers. Many half-marathons now have more female participants than male. We take that for granted in North America, but it's one of the qualities that separates our world from others.

In 2013, the Gaza marathon was cancelled when the ruling Hamas administration banned women from the race. Rather than allow the event to proceed with only men running, the organizers scrapped the entire event.

Progress can be fleeting, and we should never assume that once achieved, it can't be lost again. The Gaza event had twice been staged with women running side-by-side with men. Of the 551 Palestinians who were registered to run in 2013, 266 were women. That's 48 percent. But it quickly dropped to zero.

A 30-year-old schoolteacher who had run the 2012 edition said she had faced harassment while training, but that wasn't going to stop her from running again. "I decided to do it and not pay attention," she told the Guardian newspaper. Unfortunately, the opportunity to defy her critics was taken away.

Many of us talk about the feeling of freedom we experience when we run. But running doesn't just make you feel free; it demonstrates freedom. It's an indicator of peace and prosperity and equality, on an individual basis and a national level. At what other moment in human history and in what other place than the developed world would so many people have the time or the inclination to train for a long-distance race purely to test themselves?

We're lucky to live in a time and place in which men and women have the freedom to run. As the women of Gaza and so many other places know, it shouldn't be taken for granted. Running for exercise is a First World phenomenon. To be in a position in which the problem is not getting enough physical activity instead of too much is a statement of wealth and progress. So blessed are many of us that we must seek out the hardship and adversity that our ancestors and many people in other places could never avoid. How lucky we are to be testing ourselves because the world doesn't do it for us.

## PART 3

# THE UNLIKELY RUNNER

*"The miracle isn't that I finished. The miracle is that I had the courage to start."*

**JOHN BINGHAM**

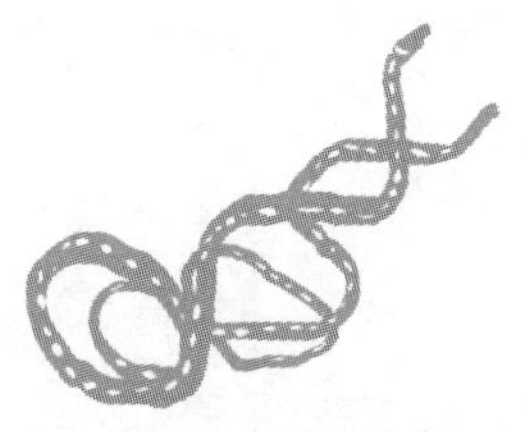

# CHAPTER 13

On a typical afternoon at my high school, there were dozens of teenagers racing around the track or running up and down the field, practicing soccer or football. I was not one of them.

Sports and exercise were not big priorities for my family. We didn't lead an unhealthy lifestyle; my mom, my older sister and I would sometimes go off on a family bike ride during summer holidays and my father walked in some long-distance fundraising events when I was a toddler, back when you collected pledges on a clipboard and went back and collected the money after you accomplished your feat. I remember him arriving home from one forty-mile pilgrimage covered in a layer of dirt. Unless my memory is playing tricks on me, he had on the same pair of shoes he wore every day to the office.

I played a lot outside when I was a child, in the backyard or at the park across the street, at a time when there were limitless hours of unsupervised activity. So I ran around a great deal, but apart from a few years of little league baseball, I wasn't involved in any organized sports.

The main priority in my household was academics. My sister excelled at school and the expectation was that I would do the same. We were both taught to read at the age of three. We were often reminded by our dad, who moved away from home and across the Atlantic as a teenager, got a job three days after arriving, and went to night school to get two degrees, about the importance of an education.

About a month into first grade, the principal came to my classroom and collected me. Despite what some of my classmates must have thought, I wasn't in trouble. What happened next wasn't a reprimand or punishment, but something that changed the course of my life. I was being skipped ahead one year. I crossed the hallway and was introduced to a new teacher and a new classroom. I don't blame school administrators or my parents – it wasn't unusual then for kids to be moved ahead if they were good at math and reading. But I wouldn't wish it for my own children.

I was incredibly shy and introverted, a bit small for my age, and on course to being a late bloomer, so from that day until a growth spurt in my mid-teens, I was almost always the smallest kid in my class, shorter than all the boys and girls and an unlikely candidate for any school sports team (or as a partner at any junior high school dance). My main aspiration in life for several years was simply to be taller.

I wasn't quite Doogie Howser, the teenaged doctor from the TV show who was way ahead of his years and constantly out of his element. But I was destined to be characterized, by others and in my own mind, as a shrimp, a scrawny, brainy, socially awkward nerd rather than a star athlete or even simply a well-adjusted kid who quietly fit in.

In the third and fourth grade, I shared a classroom with a boy who had been held back at least two years. His father was a legendary bouncer at a local nightclub; his epic battles against rowdy patrons were routinely documented in the newspaper. The boy towered over me and the rest of the class. While most of us were still watching cartoons, he was dating the girls and fighting the boys from the junior high school around the corner.

When he arrived at my next-door neighbor's house one night to take out their teenaged daughter, I happened to be looking out the window. The next day at school he threatened to blow up our family vehicle if I "spied" on him again. I was too young to read his bluff and too embarrassed to tell anyone, so for months he continued to torment me until he finally gave up and moved on to someone else.

As a child, you don't rationally account for the differences in your size and physical skills as the product of an enforced age gap. Your peers are simply the people you're around every day, so I generally forgot that I was a year younger than everyone else. I quickly came to think of myself as small and uncoordinated. My lot in life was to be spectator, not participant. I became a passionate sports fan, and while

I dreamed of being a major league baseball player – I pretended to steal second base repeatedly in our basement and I practiced my defense by throwing a tennis ball against the wall of our house for hours at a time – I rarely tried out for any sports teams.

The old-fashioned pedagogical practices of the time didn't help. I remember a high-school phys-ed unit on football that concluded with a very straightforward final test. There would be no questions about the rules or offensive and defensive strategies. Instead, our entire grade for the section would result from an exercise in which we would each stand about ten yards from the teacher and he would fire twenty passes in our direction. For each one we caught, we'd get five points. Somehow I managed to hang on to seven of these bullets; I escaped with a mark of 35 and a dozen bruises on my forearms and chest.

In all of our schoolyard activities, I was routinely the last one picked, a pattern that etched fault lines into my self-confidence for years to come. In seventh grade, I weighed about seventy-five pounds. My posture was weak, my chest almost concave. I had a great fear of taking my shirt off for swimming lessons or in the change room before phys ed. When we were divided up into shirts and skins for a basketball game, I would pray to every available god to be chosen for the shirts side. My lack of confidence became the subject of family discussions; my grandparents offered to pay for me to take martial arts classes in hopes that they might help build my self-esteem and overcome my timidity.

Throughout my school days, my only extracurricular activities were spelling bees, math competitions, and a televised high-school quiz show called *Reach for the Top*. So while my classmates were burning off calories and testing their physical limits, I was cooped up with three or four other students in a classroom on the third floor of our high school where our coach, a teacher named Mrs. Lawrence, fired trivia questions at us. I fared better on those than on the football passes.

In Grade 11, a classmate named Chris Worswick announced he was planning to run our hometown marathon. I remember being surprised that anyone I knew could attempt such a monumental task.

From my teenaged perspective, a marathon was a feat of mythic proportions, a Herculean deed achievable only by the physically gifted. That perception spoke not only to the smaller number of people running marathons at the time, but to my own skewed outlook that saw the world as divided into athletes and non-athletes – with me clearly in the second category.

I asked Chris a lot of questions about the marathon and his training, the kinds of inquiries all runners receive from innocent novices. How far do you have to run? How fast will you go? Will you try to win? I briefly considered taking up running myself and made one or two amateur attempts. I knew nothing about pacing myself and simply ran as hard as I could for as long as I could. A few hundred yards later, I was completely winded and I turned around and walked home.

Only a few years later, a photo of me at the finish line of a marathon made the front page of our daily newspaper. But I was holding a microphone and not a gold medal. I had gone to work as a sports reporter at a local radio station that provided live coverage of the annual marathon. The photo showed agony on the winner's face and earnestness on mine, as I prepared to question him about the experience.

Having covered a marathon from start to finish, I briefly considered training for the following year's event. This time I didn't even get out the door. But I must have mentioned something about it to a few people, because, not long after, another journalist told me he and some others were planning to go to New York for the marathon that fall. Would I be interested in joining them? Sure, I said. I assumed they intended to watch or cover the event. A few days later, he sent me an application form.

I never filled it out, of course. It wasn't until a dozen years later that I finally ran more than a couple of blocks.

# CHAPTER 14

During my scrawny youth, it seemed no matter what I ate, I never gained any weight. When I was sixteen, I went on a trip with an older friend, as a youth delegate to a policy forum (long before my travels involved destination races); as the only condition of her approval, my mother, who worried that I never got enough to eat, made my friend promise that I would have a proper breakfast every morning. He still teases me about the morning we slept in and I demanded that we get some food on the way to the conference, wailing "I'm too thin! I'm too thin!"

Naturally, all of that changed in my twenties. A slower metabolism, a desk job and a fondness for fast food conspired to add thirty or forty pounds to my slight frame. For a couple of years, I worked at a small newspaper where the editorial department was on the second floor. One day I ran up the stairs to get back to my desk (probably after getting some lemon tarts from the canteen truck that drove through the parking lot twice a day) and felt an unfamiliar sensation in my chest. It wasn't heart palpations or sharp pain. No, my breasts were jiggling.

I never felt like I was significantly overweight, and I did a few things I thought were helping me stay in shape, like playing a weekly game of squash with a friend. So I never reached a point at which I thought my health was in jeopardy. I just crossed the line from a little bit too thin to a little bit too heavy.

When I approached thirty, I read something in a self-help book about how in order to be successful you needed to be proactive in all areas of your life. When it came to your health, the author suggested, you didn't want to wait for the doctor to tell you to get in shape after a medical emergency. You were a lot better off avoiding a crisis than responding to one. So I decided to start doing the bare minimum of exercising three times a week, for thirty minutes at a time.

This consisted of getting up early and going to the local YMCA to ride an exercise bike before work. To help pass the time, I grabbed the newspaper on the way out my front door and read it while I pedalled, preparing for the daily radio show I was hosting. So let's just say it didn't exactly have the intensity of a spin class.

Before long, I was bored with the stationary bike and decided to try the stair-climber and then the treadmill. I've since become more accustomed to treadmill running and do it about once a week. But at the time, I couldn't imagine anything more punishing and tedious.

Now that I've learned a little about the history of the treadmill, it makes more sense. The device wasn't created for our modern aerobic convenience, to let us escape bad weather and burn some calories while binge-watching *Breaking Bad*.

It turns out the treadmill was invented almost 200 years ago as a correctional tool for prisoners. Given that synonyms for the word include chore, labor, routine, drudgery, toil, slog, and grindstone, perhaps we shouldn't be surprised.

According to a fascinating TED-Ed video, in early nineteenth-century England – a location and era that wouldn't rate highly on TripAdvisor for time travelers – convicts doing hard labor were set up on a giant paddlewheel that forced them to continue climbing. The gears they turned, sometimes for six hours straight, pumped water or crushed grain – and, no doubt, a few spirits.

Now you know why it can feel so much like torture: it was designed that way. A prison guard once described the benefits of the punitive device for his charges: "The monotonous steadiness, and not its severity, constitutes its terror." From the perspective of someone who had never run before, churning away on a gym treadmill in a novice attempt to get in shape, that sounds about right.

Those early treadmill runs certainly felt like hard labor to me. The machines seemed designed to have contrasting effects on my heart rate and the passage of time. I'd stare out at the rest of the gym, gasping for breath, keeping my eyes away from the display for as long as possible, thinking (hoping) five or ten minutes had passed, only to look down and discover I'd been moving for about ninety seconds.

In those days, I didn't dream of crossing the finish line of a marathon, but of sitting down. I remember thinking if I'd been told I had only six months to live, I'd head immediately to the nearest treadmill, just to make whatever time I had left pass as slowly as possible.

My lack of knowledge about the history of these torture devices did nothing to diminish the feeling of punishment. So, having had enough of literally going nowhere fast, I started running outdoors.

# CHAPTER 15

In the primitive days of the late twentieth century, before GPS devices, iPads, and Google Maps, when cell phones were used to make calls and you needed a tripod to take a picture of yourself, there were two ways to measure a running course. You got in your car, reset the odometer, and drove the route, or you took out a piece of string and measured on a map.

Neither one was particularly precise, but in 1998 I was striving for a basic amount of exercise, not a high level of accuracy. Using some combination of the two methods, I charted a couple of three-mile routes through my neighborhood. My goal was purely to get off the cruel treadmill to achieve my rudimentary thirty minutes of exercise a few times a week.

Nothing about the experience was pleasurable. I could never get my breathing right. I felt pangs in my sides as I gasped and wheezed my way through the ordeal. I remember asking a friend who was an experienced runner why my shins hurt so much. Was that just part of the torment of running, or was I doing something wrong? He assured me that after some time, my body would adjust and the pain would go away. I didn't believe him.

I had no intention of entering any races, let alone running a marathon. My goal was to run for thirty minutes, three times a week. What possible reason could I have for going even a minute longer?

Gradually, running became more bearable. But it was still exercise, something I recorded in my notes as "jogging" for the next couple of years. And then one day I was out for a typical three-mile run, and wondered whether I could do six. I had heard about some ten-kilometer races, and was curious whether I could run that far. So at the end of a normal run, I did a second lap. It wasn't easy, but when I finished, I was thrilled. I had run farther than ever before.

After that, I went back to running three miles at a time. But a year later, I started to wonder again if I could tackle something bigger. I was seeing more and more people running in my neighborhood and training for rapidly growing local events. So I entered a popular half-marathon and started preparing for it, adding a mile or two to my long run every week. The increments were challenging, but I managed to pull it off. I was still a complete novice, with no knowledge about training and no fancy gear or shoes. I ran the race in a cotton t-shirt and shorts along with a cap from the Baseball Hall of Fame.

I must have enjoyed that experience, because the following year I decided to double it. There was something validating about having conquered a physical challenge when I always thought of myself as a nerdy wimp. So, why not take it to the next level? If other people could run a marathon, why couldn't I?

I figured I could start training for a marathon, and if it started to feel like too much, I could always switch back to the half-marathon. I joined a clinic at the local running store. It was fun to train with a group, but the long runs were exhausting. The clinic met at 8:30 on Sunday mornings. There was a brief talk and then the various pace groups began heading out the door, starting with the fastest. Since I was in one of the slower groups, I often didn't start running until almost 9:00. The clinic leaders were terrific; sometimes they even set up an aid station at the halfway point, with water, fruit and cookies. But everything added time to the overall experience. Take a twenty-mile run at a deliberately slow pace, throw in a walk break every ten minutes (as the clinic prescribed) and the occasional stop for refreshments, and you could end up being out there for more than four hours.

By the time I finished my run, collapsed on the doorstep of the store, did a bit of stretching, drank some water and drove home, it was often 1:00. I was so exhausted I needed a nap. A Sunday morning long run was actually an experience that wiped out almost an entire day.

But somehow I managed to stick to it. I finished all the long runs. I did hills and speed work. I learned about gels and hydration. I put my faith in the process: if I did everything that was asked of me during the training, then I should get the result I wanted on race day. My only goal was to finish. I thought back to my friend in high school almost twenty years earlier. I wanted to be like him, someone who had run a marathon.

The morning of my first marathon, I woke up two hours before the alarm clock with my heart racing. In the days leading up to the race, I had told myself I was ready and there was nothing to worry about, but obviously I was more anxious than I realized. From then until I left the house, I was jumpy and restless, double-checking that I had everything I needed, worrying about the weather and wondering whether I would return home happy or disappointed.

Once the race began, I felt more relaxed. All I had left to do was run. I moved at a very conservative pace and took regular walk breaks. I drank as much water and Gatorade as I could. Even so, I can vividly remember the point at which I started wondering whether I would make it. It was on a hill with about six miles left in the race. I stopped to walk more frequently, each time reminding myself that I only had to do this once to meet my goal. The last three miles were incredibly challenging, but with a bit of willpower, I managed to cross the finish line in about four hours and seven minutes.

I remember feeling relief, but also a lot of joy. The marathon had always seemed like an impossible task, and now I had done it. Whether or not I realized it at the time, I was hooked. Running was about to become a big part of my life.

# CHAPTER 16

At the finish line of that first marathon, I ran into a friend who was a prolific runner. "You don't have to decide now if want to run another marathon," he told me. But I think I already knew I'd be back again. I ran marathons the next two springs. And then in the fall of 2006, I ran Boston, sort of.

In those days, I was barely within an hour of my Boston qualifying time. So getting into the annual race on Patriots' Day was as likely as starring in the next Indiana Jones movie. But I had started contributing a weekly column about running to the daily newspaper where I worked, and I was looking for new adventures both to experience and to write about. I had already signed up for the New York City Marathon in November. And then I stumbled upon an article about Dean Karnazes.

Karnazes is one of those superhuman figures who seems to have no limits to stamina. When I was still struggling to get to the finish line of a marathon, Karnazes was piling up one astonishing achievement after another. He once ran 350 miles continuously, going three nights without sleep. He won the Badwater Ultramarathon, a 135-mile race across Death Valley in the middle of the summer. The organizers of that race advise you to run on the painted lines on the shoulder of the road, so the pavement doesn't melt your shoes.

Starting in September of 2006, he undertook an incredible test of both endurance and logistics. He decided to run a marathon in every U.S. state, on consecutive days. So, fifty days, fifty states, fifty marathons. Most of us can't even imagine traveling to fifty states in fifty days, let alone running twenty-six miles each day before we pack up and move on.

In some states, Karnazes planned to run in a scheduled marathon, alongside hundreds or even thousands of others. For example, the last stop on his tour would be the New York City Marathon. But there aren't a lot of marathons run on weekdays. There just aren't fifty marathons conveniently spread out over fifty days in the fall. So in many cities he visited he intended to simply run the marathon course on his own.

In those cases, he invited people to join him. Up to fifty people could sign up to run with Dean in each of the cities where there wasn't an official race. I decided to join him for one stop on the tour, his twenty-ninth run, which just happened to be in Boston.

On Sunday, October 15, 2006, about four dozen of us gathered in the historic town of Hopkinton, where thousands of runners fill up every square inch of space at the start of the Boston Marathon. For that one day in April, Hopkinton is hopping. But this was one of the other 364 days each year, when the population is about 14,000, not 50,000. It seemed very quaint and very quiet.

After a quick introduction from Karnazes, we were off down the hill that every runner talks about after the start of the race. It was a crisp and clear autumn day, perfect running weather, and the fall colors made for a spectacular start to the run. I remarked to another runner that the bright leaves were something unique to our experience, something Boston Marathon participants would not get to witness in the spring.

For a man on a mission, Karnazes was incredibly social. He bounced around the pack of runners, acting as host and leader, offering water and food and trying to learn as much about each of us as he could. Perhaps after running in solitude so often, he was glad for the company.

When we got a chance to talk, I asked him why he was running a marathon every day. At first he joked, "I don't have a car," but then said he was concerned about the rising rate of obesity and wanted to draw attention to physical fitness. The money he raised from sponsors and participants like me would go to his foundation, which promotes physical activity for children.

But I suspected that was only a small part of the motivation. Guys like Dean Karnazes are driven by a desire to test their limits, to do something that's never been done. There's something in all of us that wants to blow people away, to make their eyes widen and, to make them say, "You did what?" For many of us, a marathon is enough. But someone like Karnazes needs to go further. That he attaches himself to a cause is admirable and makes the whole thing worthwhile. But he's running for the same reason all of us do, just on a larger, more remarkable scale.

There was one woman in the group who, that day, was completing her hundredth marathon. There was a man who was doing his first.

He told the story of a runner from Japan who had joined him the previous month in Hawaii. The man was on his honeymoon, and was running with Karnazes to prove he was worthy to his new wife. Karnazes asked him if he was tired from his wedding night. "Oh no," the man said. "I saved myself for the marathon."

At the halfway point of the race, we were joined by a group of runners from the cross-country running team from Wellesley, the women's college famous for its scream tunnel on Marathon Monday. One of the new runners asked, "Which one of you is Dean?" About four of the runners replied, "I am." Thanks to the new runners with fresh legs, the pace picked up in the second half.

When we got to Newton, Karnazes fell to the ground and said, "I can't take Heartbreak Hill." Of course, he was not in any pain at all. He was only hamming it up for a laugh. A second later, he jumped to his feet and sprinted ahead to catch up with the front end of the group.

We crossed the finish line, still painted on the road six months after the last race, after just under four hours of running. It would be years before qualifying for the real race would become something I could even attempt, so I was pleased to have simply found a way to run the Boston Marathon course.

A few minutes later, I glanced at Dean and noticed he didn't seem to have broken a sweat. We would both be running the New York City Marathon exactly three weeks later. The only difference was that he would be completing another twenty marathons in between.

# CHAPTER 17

Depending on how you look at it, for the first decade of my running career I was either too slow or too young to qualify for the Boston Marathon. While tens of thousands of athletes reached the Holy Grail for amateur runners each year, I was watching at home. But long before I came even close to qualifying myself, I was able to play a small part in a Boston story.

I have been blessed with the good fortune of having a friend who runs at roughly the same pace as I do. Bob happens to be about ten years older than I am, so running at our speed, he's always been a lot closer to hitting his Boston-qualifying time than I have been.

A few years ago, when we ran together only occasionally, Bob tried to qualify for Boston and came up a few minutes short. I ran another marathon around the same time and was reminded once again that until I aged a decade or so, Boston was out of reach.

So what would be my next goal? If I couldn't get to Boston myself, I decided I should strive for the next-best thing. On a routine run not long after our respective marathons, I threw out an idea: Bob and I would train for a marathon together with the goal of finishing in his Boston-qualifying time. It would give me an excuse to train for another marathon, to aim for a specific time that might even turn out to be my best ever. And if all went well, he'd get into Boston and I'd congratulate him for doing so.

We started our quest in 2007. Our goal seemed realistic and our training typically went well, but something always got in the way. First, Bob broke his collarbone on a bike ride, putting him on the disabled list for a couple of months – he had to sleep in a chair for a few weeks – and cancelling our next planned race.

The following winter our training got off to a great start. We did almost every run together and stayed on course through tempo runs, speed work and long runs. Along the way, we talked our way through the plans for what would become his next best-selling book and my latest business venture.

We ran together so often it became, well, a running joke. Each of our wives started saying, "It's your boyfriend" when the phone rang. We were just slightly ahead of the times. The bromance comedy *I Love You, Man* was still a year away (for the record, we did not go see it together).

All signs were pointing to a successful marathon. But three weeks before race day, on the eve of our last long training run before the race, Bob noticed he was having some trouble with his breathing. After a few tests, he learned from his doctor that he had an infection in his heart. It wasn't quite as serious as that sounds, but there was to be no running for at least a few months. Once again, our race, and his dream, were cancelled.

Our plan had been to run a marathon in the Toronto area in early May. Throughout our training, I had always pictured running it together, so when he pulled out, I almost did the same. For one thing, we were supposed to travel there together, and I didn't feel like making the trip on my own. But he convinced me to go ahead. I had other reasons to be at the event – we were launching a new magazine for runners called *iRun* – and so I went ahead and spent two days handing out copies of the brand-new publication at the race expo.

Yes, I was on my feet constantly for the two days before the race. I went into marathon morning with very low expectations. Bob's qualifying time was three hours and thirty-five minutes, so our goal was to run as close to three-and-a-half hours as possible. I figured I would just stay on that pace – which is almost exactly eight minutes per mile – for as long as I could and then see what happened.

Somehow, the miles kept piling up and I didn't lose any steam. At twenty-four miles, I started to get some cramps in my legs, but I figured I would just hang on as long as I could. At twenty-five miles, I was struggling but still going. At twenty-six miles, I looked down at my watch and realized that I had a legitimate chance to break 3:30.

I have no idea from where I summoned the energy, given that five minutes earlier I had thought I had nothing left. But I ran as hard as I could to the finish line, and hit my watch right after I crossed.

The watch said 3:30:01. But something told me I had hit my watch just after the finish line, not right at it. I waited for the official results and discovered I had finished in 3:29:59.1, nine-tenths of a second under my target. That didn't get either Bob or me into Boston, but it proved our training could produce the result he needed. And it was my fastest marathon so far.

That fall, we ramped up our training again. And this time, finally, we made it to the starting line together. On race day, we made a deal. If he hit a wall, I would stay with him and try to pull him along to the finish. But if I started struggling, he would go ahead without me. We ran together for twenty miles, then I started getting more of those painful leg cramps. This time they came earlier and were a lot more debilitating. Over the next few miles, I watched him get farther and farther ahead, disappointed to be falling behind, but satisfied to see that he was still on pace.

I struggled on, and with a mile to go, I learned he had made it with a few minutes to spare. I had only one goal for the race, and we had made it. My only disappointment was that I didn't cross the finish line with him. But after I hobbled in a few minutes later, we celebrated with our families for the rest of the day.

When I used to run by myself, I often pictured striding to the finish line of a race, feeling strong and crossing in a fast time. But once we started training together, with a new goal in mind, my vision of that final stretch changed. I pictured a celebration in the final few hundred yards, during which I would point out loudly to my friend that he was finally, after several false starts and years of training, on the verge of making his goal.

I figured eventually I might get my own shot at running the most coveted marathon of all. But even if that didn't happen, it was still a milestone for me that my running buddy achieved his goal, reaching the end of a long journey we had begun together almost three years before.

If only I had been able to shout to him what I planned if we crossed the finish line together: *Bob, you're going to run the Boston Marathon.*

# CHAPTER 18

When I turned thirty, I was the chief executive of a media start-up with about sixty employees. I had just started doing minimal exercise at the gym, and I certainly wasn't a runner. And yet when my co-workers got me a cake for my milestone birthday, it had the words "Marathon Man" on it.

Although the frosting now seems very prophetic, the message was chosen for a different reason. I was known for a much different obsession, one that was quite the opposite of running. At the end of most workdays, I would walk down the hall to the creative department and play video games with the production artists. One of my favorite games was called Marathon.

By the time I turned forty, I had run six marathons, I was writing a weekly column about running in the local daily newspaper, and I had launched a running magazine called *iRun*. My wife produced a video for my birthday party in which many friends delivered their best wishes and teased me about getting older. A handful of them talked about how it was about time I tried to get into Boston.

Boston was definitely on my mind, so much so that it showed up in a magazine column I wrote in which I created a runner's bucket list. Some people, of course, list running a marathon as one of the things they want to do before they die. But as a runner with many dreams, I figured it would be amusing to draft a bucket list just for running.

Itemizing your goals can provide a little bit of extra motivation to keep going, to keep thinking, "What's next?" when you cross a finish line. It can establish a blueprint to motivate you not just to challenge yourself with another race, but to fulfill other creative and entertaining goals.

I've since ticked a few of the boxes, like completing the Goofy – a half-marathon and marathon on consecutive days – at the Walt

Disney World Marathon in Florida, and serving as a pace bunny for the marathon in my hometown, Ottawa.

I threw on my runner's bucket list a bunch of races that I still would like to tackle sometime in the future: the majestic London Marathon, because it looks like an amazing race and it's an excuse to go back to one of my favorite cities in the world. The Big Sur Marathon, because it's an incredibly challenging and also astonishingly scenic route. Chicago, Berlin and Rome all look like very appealing marathons to me. The Around the Bay 30k race in Hamilton, Ontario, which is older than even the Boston Marathon.

There are a couple of marathons that start in one country and finishing in another. Someday I hope to complete either the Niagara Falls International Marathon or the Detroit Marathon, which crosses into Windsor, Ontario. Or maybe even both.

I'm not sure I'll ever become one of those runners who routinely does fifty-mile or multi-stage events, but I'd like to do an ultramarathon at some point in the future. I'd also like to find an incredible trail race to complete. Because I live in the heart of a city, almost all of my training is on the roads. I'd welcome an excuse to do more trail running. And I'd also like to do a relay race of some kind. I have friends who have traveled to spectacular settings and taken part in challenging team events. Maybe someday, when my kids are older, I can tick that box.

But it wasn't just about races. For example, I figure every runner who has the chance should relive the classic moment from the movie Rocky and run up the steps of the Philadelphia Museum of Art. I have this idea that it would be fun to do a long run, maybe even a half-marathon, on a cruise ship. I've been on one or two cruises and I liked the experience of doing laps while traveling across the ocean. I'd like to run on my seventieth birthday. I also tossed onto the list that I'd like to pass someone from Kenya in a race.

One of my greatest dreams is to travel in the footsteps of Terry Fox, the heroic Canadian who tried to cross the country on one leg for cancer research. Someday I will go to the place near Thunder Bay, Ontario where his run ended but his impact had only just begun.

There are other places where I aspire simply to enjoy a good run. I'd like to travel at least once more along the River Calder in Yorkshire, where my father grew up. I'd like to say I've run on every continent. I've covered three so far, but I haven't even set foot on the others. I'd like to run up the steps of the Empire State Building in New York or the CN Tower in Toronto. I'd like to spend a year in the Big Apple and run as many of the New York Road Runners events as possible, culminating in another New York City Marathon.

I'd also like to run with a few famous people who happen to be runners. I once had the chance to do a very quick five miles with bestselling author Malcolm Gladwell, who was an accomplished runner in high school and is now turning in some amazing times as a masters athlete. There are lots of other fascinating people I'd welcome the chance to run with, like musician Jim Cuddy of Blue Rodeo or retired hockey player Daniel Alfredsson. I'd be happy just to meet Paula Radcliffe, who holds the women's world record in the marathon (I wouldn't be able to keep up with her on a run).

Someday, I hope to complete one expedition with my inspiring friend Ray Zahab. Ray is a preternatural endurance athlete and humanitarian who has run across the Sahara Desert and the Atacama Desert and journeyed to the South Pole. He also does shorter, somewhat more manageable expeditions, many of which include students, and it's one of those that I intend to join.

I hope to get the chance to pace my wife all the way through her first marathon. Ginny has run half-a-dozen half-marathons and is still contemplating the merits of running a marathon one day. I'd like to help her, unless she'd find it easier if I'm not there. I'd like to run a race with each of my kids at some point. I've done a few short runs with my son Jack. I won't put any pressure on them to become runners, but if they're interested, I'll be right there with them.

I itemized all of those goals on my runner's bucket list. At the very bottom of my list, presented almost as a cheeky afterthought, was running the Boston Marathon. But while it may have appeared last, it had probably become my top priority.

And once you put something on a list like this, it means you have to do it. So in my mind, I was now committed to Boston, even though I was still a long way off. In the meantime, I set out to achieve another ambitious target from the list, one that had nothing to do with time and everything to do with money.

# CHAPTER 19

It's hard to escape the fact that for me, running marathons is tied to loss. In 2003, I completed my first half-marathon only a few months after my only sibling, my sister Dianne, had died of a rare heart and lung condition. There were many reasons why running was changing from exercise to passion, why I made the transition from jogger to runner, but one of the principal motivations was that the longer runs and the path toward a goal were a tonic for my anxiety and grief.

The next year, my father was diagnosed with cancer and was told he had one year to live. In 2004, about halfway between the diagnosis and its eventual result, I ran my first marathon. Once again, I found refuge and purpose in the long run. When there's nothing you can do about the horrible things that are happening around you, it sometimes helps to pour yourself into something simple and productive over which you have more control. I remember many nights when I'd get home from the hospital and the only thing I could do to restore my sanity was get out and run as hard as possible.

In retrospect, I think the immediate effect on my mood and mental health was only part of the motivation for my running. On some level, I was also trying to outrun death. In those days I would lie awake at night, obsessed with questions about mortality, struggling with the finite nature of life. I needed to do something, anything, not only to ward off the demons and dark thoughts, but to make sure I was as healthy as possible, for both my mother, who deserved to be spared any further loss, and myself.

For me, every run brings me back to when I first started doing those longer runs. That new chapter in my life coincided with a dark, devastating period during which I lost half my family. Every time I run, every time I cross a finish line, it connects me to a time when my sister and father were still around to cheer me on.

I turned that first marathon into a fundraiser for the hospital that had treated both my sister and my father, and I raised about $10,000. It was a bit of a daring leap to tie my performance to a charity, since I wasn't sure I could finish the marathon. But I figured the added expectations of all my sponsors would be extra motivation in those last few miles to help me get it done. My mom and my aunt, who was visiting from England to see my father one last time, cheered me on from the sidelines.

Over the next few years, I embarked on several other fundraising efforts. I ran for the Leukemia and Lymphoma Society, for a sports program for disadvantaged youth at the YMCA, for cancer research. Fundraising is not a part of every race I enter – there are only so many times I can ask my friends and family for donations – but I try to do run for charity at least once every couple of years.

Fundraising has become one of the best aspects of our sport. In the past decade, I've talked to hundreds of runners who have collectively raised millions of dollars for medical research, community programs, and other important causes. A race is no longer just a group of people crossing a finish line and achieving a personal goal. It's become a powerful force for community good.

And it has become a teacher of life lessons. In 2012, I witnessed a powerful example of the human spirit that I will never forget. I was getting ready for another spring marathon and I had published my bucket list, which included the goal of raising $50,000 with one run. My friends at the local hospital foundation noticed that ambitious goal in my column. Being good fundraising professionals, they pounced. So all of a sudden, I had agreed to pull together five times as much as I'd ever raised with a single run.

In the advent of my first marathon, I was more worried about whether I would finish the race than hit my fundraising target. This time it was the other way around. I honestly wasn't sure whether I'd even come close. A few friends even raised their eyebrows and wished me luck. "Fifty thousand dollars?" I remember one of them asking me incredulously. But thanks to some generous friends and some listeners to my daily radio show, I got off to a good start. Just like training for a marathon, you can't hit a big fundraising target in one day. You have to keep pushing over weeks and months.

One week before the race, I had raised $33,000. That was an extraordinary number, but it meant I still had $17,000 to go. So I launched another appeal, emailing everyone I had ever known, asking for more help from my listeners and offering up prizes to donors. Something happened and the results gathered steam. With three days to go, donations jumped to just over $49,000.

That morning, I provided an update to my listeners and a few more gifts came in. Then my producer, Tom Woodward (who took up running in his fifties and has completed a few half-marathons and marathons himself) answered a call from a listener named Richard Weitzel.

Mr. Weitzel said he was almost ninety years old and was suffering from terminal cancer. He wanted to make sure I met my goal, and he asked Tom how far I was from the target.

"Six hundred and twenty-eight dollars," Tom told him.

"I'll write you a check for that right now," said Mr. Weitzel.

"That's a lot of money," Tom said.

"Well, I've been given a lot in my life," he said.

Mr. Weitzel said he knew the money wasn't going to help him, but that it might help someone else in his condition in the future. And he said he wanted to be certain that I met my goal. His check put us over the top, and it was a great story to tell on the air that inspired more people to call in. By the day of the race, we had raised more than $56,000.

Throughout the marathon, I thought about the many rewards I've received from running, and I don't mean the medals you get at the end of the race. One of the greatest gifts with which I've been blessed is being able to witness the truly selfless generosity of so many people, and Dick Weitzel became the most prominent example of that. When you're caught up in your own personal goals, like trying to run quickly, it's easy to forget how much of a privilege it is to run.

A week after the race, I paid him a visit at his home. We had a great chat. He told me about his life and his illness and that he was grateful for the loving care of the doctors and nurses and others who provide services to veterans (he'd served in the air force in World War II).

He said he wasn't strong enough for an operation and that the treatments had ended. The doctors couldn't help him anymore.

"But it could be worse," he said.

I was amazed by his perspective and his graciousness. After I had dwelled on death and struggled to find meaning for so long, it was incredibly meaningful to see someone thinking about others when confronted with his own mortality. I thanked him for donating the $628 to get me to $50,000. I told him how he had inspired me and so many others with his kindness.

From my very first half-marathon in 2003, all the way up to the Goofy at Disney World nine years later, I had kept the medals from every single race I ran. I have dozens of medals, big and small, fancy and simple, from marathons, half-marathons, triathlons and other races. They're all in a very nice display case my wife assembled for me at Christmas one year. I'm not very sentimental and I don't have a lot of keepsakes. This, however, was a special gift: my whole running career, summarized in a glass box.

But I decided under the circumstances I would make an exception. I brought out the medal from my fundraising marathon and I presented it to Mr. Weitzel. He seemed quite moved as I slipped it around his neck.

Three weeks later, Dick Weitzel passed away. Since then, he's crossed my mind dozens of times, especially when I'm running. Every once in a while, in the middle of a training run, I'll remember back to when we sat together and talked, and I'll think about how lucky I am to have met him and learned from his generosity.

When I went to pay my respects at the funeral home, I was proud to see that his family put the marathon medal right next to him. His son pointed out something I'd never considered before: the word "finisher" in large print on the ribbon. How very appropriate. Mr. Weitzel was the finisher who got me to my goal. And that's why I thought he deserved the medal more than I did.

# CHAPTER 20

In 2015, I had another chance to turn a run into something more than just a personal goal. I was the co-chair of the local United Way campaign in Ottawa, which had a fundraising target of more than $15 million. As the end of the campaign approached, we decided to plan an event that would create a big finish. I pledged to run all over the city, covering one kilometer for every $1,000 that people donated during a final blitz, with a target of $50,000. If we made it, it would be the longest run of my life, just over thirty-one miles.

Heading into the final weekend before my run, I wasn't sure I'd even come close to the target. It had the potential to be a bit of a public relations challenge if we came up significantly short. But thanks to a last-minute appeal and a groundswell of support in the final forty-eight hours, we met and exceeded the goal. There were several large contributions and an incredible number of small donations, proof of both the generosity of individuals and the power of crowds.

We planned out a route that took me to several of the agencies and programs funded by United Way donors, where the money would be deployed to change people's lives. Joined by a United Way employee named Paul, who was then training to run a Boston-qualifying time himself, I ran a total of 51.7 kilometers, just over thirty-two miles. It was almost six miles farther than I'd ever run before, but I saw only a small part of our city and only a fraction of the impact of United Way investments.

There are moments in your life when you see everyone at their best. As I traveled around the city for hours on foot, I witnessed the kindness, generosity, and hard work of hundreds of caring people. The experience was enlightening and empowering. At one stop, about halfway through the run, the attendant from a nearby parking lot approached us. His name was Juan, and it's a safe bet that he was a relative newcomer to the city. Juan had heard about the run on the radio and wanted to do his part. He enthusiastically handed over forty dollars. It reminded me that for generous people, giving is an opportunity, not an obligation.

As I journeyed from place to place, I certainly observed many of the challenges our society faces. In cities, more demands are being placed on social agencies than ever before. There was even a medical emergency happening at one of the agencies as we visited. But what resonated with me every step of the way was not the size of the obstacles we face, but the energy, enthusiasm and creativity behind every effort to remove them.

It's easy to get discouraged by news headlines about homelessness, gun violence, and mental health issues, among many other matters faced by growing urban centers. Such challenges are frustratingly persistent, and their solutions aren't simple. But each of us has a choice: gripe at the futility of it all, or join and support those who are doing something about it, changing the lives of others through their thoughtfulness and hard work.

Indeed, the more time you spend with the people who care for and support the most vulnerable among us, the more you believe in what's possible. And if you're going to set ambitious goals for yourself, in running or in any other part of life, it helps to have that perspective reinforced.

I was grateful for all the support I received before and during my run. It was truly one of the best days of my life. The finish was as thrilling as any marathon. It's great to have personal running goals like qualifying for the Boston Marathon, but when you turn your training into something that's about more than you, something that will genuinely do some good in the community, it becomes truly special. You might strive to change your own life through running, but nothing will match the value or the reward of changing someone else's at the same time.

I also realized that day that it's pretty easy to be a volunteer, to dabble in community service and to chip in a bit of time and money here and there. Even reaching out to my friends and family and promising to run far in exchange for donations is not that difficult.

The real heroes are those who work every day at United Way and other community agencies, foundations, and initiatives, the people who dedicate their working lives to raising the money and delivering the programs that make our community safer and better. The day after our run, for example, Paul went back to work in his role researching and evaluating the United Way's community investments. These superstars face conditions far more difficult than a long run. And they rarely get the credit and attention I received for my fundraising effort.

An accomplishment like a marathon pales in comparison to the work that so many people do to make our world a better place. It's for these heroes that I dedicate myself to community service, and in their honor that I run and raise money. Compared to theirs, my commitment is small. And thanks to them, my rewards have been infinitely disproportionate to my effort.

# CHAPTER 21

In September of 2012, I ran what was then the fastest marathon of my life. In the omnipresent context of Boston, the result was either a little too slow, a little too early or a little too late. Even so, it set the stage for a new chapter in my quest for Boston. Having come much closer than ever before, I would now start to take qualifying much more seriously.

I wasn't necessarily expecting to run at a fast pace. The last time I'd run a marathon with the goal of going as fast as possible was three years earlier when I finished the Green Mountain Marathon in Vermont in 3:31:08, about a minute slower than my personal record. My friend Bob ran that one too, and qualified for Boston a second time.

In the next two-and-a-half years, I ran six more marathons, none of which was particularly fast. At this point, I was so far off from my Boston qualifying time – then three hours and twenty minutes – that it didn't seem realistic. Instead, I was running for pleasure and ticking off the boxes on my bucket list.

First, I organized a solo fundraising run in September 2010. A friend of mine had run fifty kilometers on the day she turned fifty. I was inspired by how she connected her age to a distance, but I didn't want to wait that long or run that far. So I figured why not a marathon – 42.2 kilometers – on the day I turned 42.2 years old. Twenty percent of a year is exactly seventy-three days, so I added that to my forty-second birthday. It happened to fall on a Saturday, which made it very convenient. I raised money for the Leukemia and Lymphoma Society and ran a marathon on my metric marathon birthday.

That fall, I ran the New York City Marathon for the second time, and this time Bob joined me. It was another great experience, but it wasn't a race in which I could count on going fast. We ran the whole race together and thoroughly enjoyed the experience. The next year, I planned to run the Marine Corps Marathon in Washington with Bob. Again, we weren't aiming to go fast. So a month before the race, I decided to tack on a local race and run two marathons three weeks apart. Needless to say, neither one was quick.

In January 2012, I ran the Goofy, the Disney event from my bucket list in which you run a half-marathon on Saturday and a marathon on Sunday. It was a phenomenal experience, and I met my goal of breaking two hours and four hours in the two races. Finally, in May of 2012, I ran the race for which I raised $50,000 and served as a pace bunny, ticking another box on my list.

A couple of things made me decide to run another marathon that year. For one, I wanted to check how fast I could go if I trained hard again, to find out where my capacity was as I approached my mid-forties. The training for the Goofy had made me feel strong. In preparing for that double race, I had completed long training runs every Saturday and Sunday. I felt like those double runs made my endurance better than ever before. I wanted to see what would happen if I kept up the twin training runs that I did for the Goofy, but then didn't run a half-marathon the day before the marathon. Would the extra preparation increase my endurance so I had more strength in the second half of the race, so I was less likely to struggle through those grueling final few miles?

Beyond that, I felt inspired by my experience of raising more than $50,000 – and witnessing the generosity of Dick Weitzel – to think that anything was possible if I put my mind to it.

So I entered an evening marathon in late summer, a small race tacked on to the tail end of an iron-distance triathlon. My goal was simply to go out and run as well as I could. I thought if it went well, I might get within range of my fastest time, but I wasn't expecting a record.

At the start, the temperature was a little warmer than I hoped, so I wasn't sure if a fast time would be possible. But it turned out to be a perfect night. It was the first time I'd run a marathon with the temperature cooling rather than rising as the race progressed. The run consisted of eight loops of about three miles and a quarter. A lot of runners find loop courses monotonous, but I don't mind them. To me, they are simple and straightforward. Instead of thinking about how many miles I had completed, I just counted the loops I had done. And I saw many of the same spectators and volunteers over and over again, which gave me lots of encouragement.

Sometimes, running feels like a grind. But early in this race, moving quickly felt more effortless than usual. Of course, in a marathon you can be flying along at fifteen miles and walking at twenty. But I just kept focusing on completing the next loop. With one lap to go, I suddenly started to think a quick time was achievable. A friend who had guided the leaders on his bike circled back and found me. He encouraged me on the slight hills and brought me all the way to the final hundred yards.

I crossed the finish line in 3:27:12, almost three minutes faster than my previous record, which I had run more than four years (and ten marathons) earlier. It was a thrilling moment and I pumped my fist enthusiastically as I approached the finish line and saw the clock.

About a week later, on my first run after the race, my training buddy Bob congratulated me on the race and said, "That's very encouraging!" Bob, of course, was thinking about Boston.

I remember thinking: *Encouraging? I just ran the best race of my life. And I'm not exactly a young man any more.* No, this was more than encouraging. It was exhilarating, blissful, delightful. It was a moment to celebrate. I might never run this fast again. Sure, I was still determined to get to that famous starting line in Hopkinton. But it has never been all about Boston for me. Even if I never ran a faster marathon, I told myself, I wouldn't be disappointed with a personal best.

Nevertheless, I have to admit that it was hard to view this improved time without connecting it to my long-term goal. Every time you run a fast marathon, you instinctively connect it to your qualifying standard. If I was a couple of years older, then a 3:27 marathon would have been enough to meet the current requirement for a man my age.

Under normal circumstances, it would have been very encouraging. All that would be necessary would be for me to get a bit older and maintain my pace. Unfortunately, however, as I approached this new age category, the demand for Boston was growing and the organizers had already announced the rules would change. Qualifying for Boston was about to get a lot tougher.

It was still a daunting prospect. But once I saw that I had the capacity to go faster, I was resolute that this wouldn't be my fastest marathon for very long. What was once out of reach was now much more within striking distance. My quest for Boston was about to get a lot more intense.

# CHAPTER 22

Once upon a time, you didn't have to qualify for the Boston Marathon. Until 1970, you could register for Boston just like any other race. You could even choose it as your first marathon, without proving yourself in a previous event.

But from 1960 to 1969, the size of the Boston field increased by almost sevenfold, from 197 participants to 1,342. Believe it or not, the organizers worried that a field of more than a thousand would lead to an overly congested course. Imagine if they knew one day more than 30,000 would gather in Hopkinton every April.

In 1970, runners had to submit a certification from a coach, indicating "he has trained sufficiently to finish the course in less than four hours." Although women had run Boston, they were still a couple of years away from being officially welcomed, so there was no need for gender-neutral language.

There was also no attempt to make Boston welcoming and friendly to slower runners. Rather snobbishly, the 1970 application stated, "This is not a jogging race." Remember, the goal was to attract fewer runners, not more.

Despite the snooty message and the lofty cut-off time, the field still wasn't culled to the desired number. In 1970, 1,174 runners entered the race. So just a year later, the time was dropped to three hours and thirty minutes, and the requirement was not evidence that you had trained for that time, but that you'd completed another race. You could use a marathon, or a race of ten, fifteen or twenty miles, to justify your Boston entry.

Those times stood for the next six years, with the women who joined the field starting in 1972 held to exactly the same standard as the men. In 1977, the times were tightened even further. Men under forty had to run a qualifying marathon in less than three hours.

Women of all ages had to do 3:05 and men forty and over had to run better than 3:30.

By 1979, there were 7,927 registrants, up forty percent from the previous year. The times were adjusted again so that men nineteen to thirty-nine years of age had to run 2:50, while older men had to hit 3:10. The numbers were further tweaked in the years ahead, with more age categories added. But the bar was still very high and the resulting level of participation, at least compared to more recent numbers, relatively low.

In 1987, the marathon attracted new levels of sponsorship. That helped attract more volunteers, a more professional race organization and, presumably, a desire to have as many people experience the event (and appreciate the sponsors) as possible. The organizers figured they could accommodate almost 10,000 runners, so for the first time in years, the qualifying times were relaxed. Men under thirty-nine needed to break three hours. For each successive decade from forty and up, men were given an extra ten minutes. Women received exactly thirty minutes more than the men in each age group.

Just three years later, the numbers were changed again. This time the fastest qualifying time, for men eighteen to thirty-four years old, was 3:10. The age categories were reduced to five years in length, and for every increment over thirty-five, you got an extra five minutes. Once again, women had an extra half-hour in each category.

Why an extra half-hour? It's not clear, but it seems somewhat arbitrary. Is the difference in capacity between a typical man and woman thirty minutes at all age levels and speeds? Is there not some logic to having a smaller gender gap for the lower age categories and a broader one for older runners?

You could get into the science of it and figure out what percentage of the world record in each age group a man or a woman has to run, or analyze the average speed of marathoners of all ages. But ultimately, all time targets are arbitrary. Is it fair that someone who is thirty-nine years and eleven months old has to run five minutes faster than a runner who has just turned forty?

In general, the qualifying times have appeared to favor women and older runners slightly. The perception was always that the older you got, the closer you would be to qualifying. There are probably more forty-five-year-old women who can break four hours than thirty-year-old men who can finish a marathon in under 3:10. If you waited long enough, and you kept running marathons, one day you would get your chance.

By 2003, the goal was to attract up to 20,000 participants. So the times in some of the older age categories were further relaxed and new, older age categories were added.

Those rules stood until 2012. With marathon participation booming and demand for Boston rising dramatically, the process was altered dramatically. Just before I entered a new age group, with a qualifying standard I thought would be within my ability, the rules were changed in several significant ways.

First, they reduced every qualifying standard by five minutes. If you once needed four hours to get into Boston, you would now have to run a 3:55. Second, they eliminated the one-minute grace period they used to provide. Until 2012, if you're qualifying standard was 3:45, you could run anything up to 3:45:59 and you would get in. Now that was gone. Effectively, the qualifying times had been reduced by a second less than six minutes.

There was another change, one of much greater consequence. Once upon a time, it was first-come, first-served for qualifiers. All you had to do to get into Boston was meet your qualifying time, even if it was by just one second; as long as you went online soon after registration opened, you were in. Sometimes it took weeks before Boston was sold out. The registration would open in September and you could run a marathon in December or January and still get in.

In 2009, the race sold out in November. Anyone who hadn't posted a qualifying time by then was shut out. The following year, it sold out in eight hours. It was starting to become like a rock concert, with people sitting by their computers waiting for the registration to open.

Boston would no longer have a registration race with runners approved in the order they applied. Now there would be a window during which any qualifier could register, and if too many people tried to get in, the organizers would drop the slowest runners. It didn't matter in what order you registered, but how fast your time was. In other words, even if you met your qualifying time, it didn't mean you'd get in. All the spots might be taken by faster runners.

I had always planned to attempt a sub-3:30 marathon when I turned forty-five. But now, under the new rules, I would have to get in under 3:25 just to be eligible to apply, and that didn't necessarily mean I would be accepted. I might have to do 3:24 or better to make the cut.

I used to think all I would have to do to get into Boston was get older. Now I had to get much faster as well. Realistically, I went from needing to run a marathon in anything under 3:30:59 to having to finish about seven minutes sooner. And I had to do it at a time when age was slowing my body down. I felt like I was Charlie Brown running up to the football, only to see Lucy, in the form of Boston Marathon officials, pull it away from me.

PART 4

# HILLS AND THUNDERSTORMS

*"When you're running…there's a little person that talks to you and that little person says 'Oh, I'm tired. My lung's about to pop. I'm so hurt. I'm so tired. There's no way I can possibly continue." And you want to quit, right? If you learn how to defeat that person when you're running you will learn how to not quit when things get hard in your life."*

**WILL SMITH**

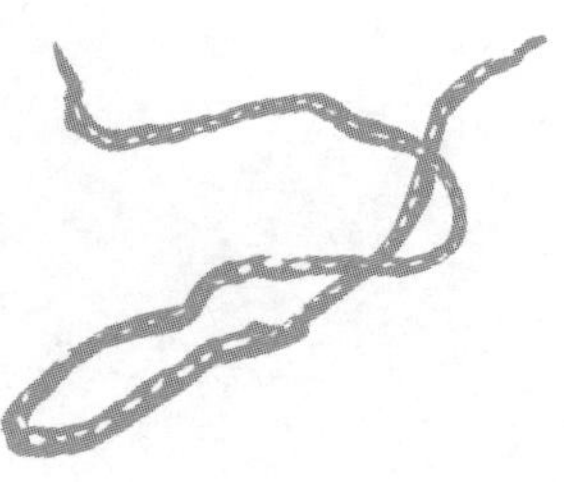

# CHAPTER 23

When was the last time you said to yourself, "If only I were older"? I'm guessing it was probably well before you turned thirty. Other than gaining wisdom and experience, there are few things people relish about aging. One of the big differences between me and my kids is that they can't wait for their next birthday.

The Boston Marathon is one exception. If you're struggling to qualify, sometimes time can be on your side. When non-runners hit a major birthday milestone, they might lament the evaporation of their youth. But runners think, "Hey – new age category!" Not only will you be ranked against a new cohort of runners when you check your results online, you also get a break on Boston qualifying standards, which are adjusted downward in five-year increments. So if you don't make it to Boston when you're thirty-nine or forty-four, just wait a year and the qualifying time will be slower.

Of course, after a certain age, there's also a risk you'll be slower too. There are many reasons why we tend to lose speed as we age. According to Alex Hutchinson, the runner, author, and journalist who writes the "Sweat Science" blog for *Runner's World*, the older we are, the less proficiently our bodies operate. Everything from our muscle strength to our efficiency at producing oxygen declines.

What's not completely clear, however, is precisely why that happens. Until recently, it was assumed to be a natural consequence of aging; lately, some scientists have begun to speculate it's at least partly because most of us are less likely to do hard exercise in our fifties than in our thirties, particularly the hard work that will keep our bodies strong and efficient.

When you're young and you take on a challenge, you have the time and the inclination to be all in. The deeper you get into your thirties, forties, and fifties, the more likely that you have big competing priorities, especially expanding work and family roles. Not only do they consume time and energy (and sometimes deprive you of precious sleep), they often present significant challenges to overcome, meaning it's less likely you'll seek out a separate, physically demanding test in your spare time. In simple terms, as you age, you become more likely to say, "I'm too old for this."

There's at least one major physical factor, a phenomenon called age-related sarcopenia. Basically, you lose muscle mass as you age, as much as one percent per year. And that has a big effect on athletic performance.

When you run, you use muscle fibers to make your legs move. But you deploy only a fraction of them at one time. So as some fibers fatigue, others kick in. When you have a lot of muscle mass, your body can move the work around to different fibers. When you lose muscle mass, there are fewer fibers to share the load. You use the same ones over and over again, so you fatigue sooner. That's why strength training seems to make a bigger difference for older runners than younger. The more muscle mass you maintain, the less likely you are to get tired quickly.

Here's the good news: you do have some control over how quickly your performance declines. With the right kind of training, you can preserve muscle mass. So you don't necessarily have to slow down at the same rate as the Boston qualifying times. The structure of those standards isn't exactly scientific anyway; there's no evidence to suggest that the average marathon runner's performance declines in convenient increments of five or ten minutes for every five years they age, nor that women at any age are typically thirty minutes slower than men. That's why it has tended to get easier to get into Boston as you get older.

But not when the bar gets raised just when you're about to enter a new age category. My clever plan had been to age gracefully into Boston, to win a war of attrition patiently and strategically by slowing down more slowly than the qualifying times – to get in by getting older. Thanks to the last-minute change in qualifying times, I had to get faster as well. In fact, unless I wanted to wait another five years, and hope that they didn't bump up the times yet again, I was going to have to run the fastest marathon of my life in my mid-forties.

What's involved in getting faster? In large part, I learned, it comes down to something called mitochondria. Like everything, your muscles are made up of cells. The powerhouses of those cells are called mitochondria. Just like the marathon, the word *mitochondrion* is of Greek origin, and means thread or granule. It's a bit of a long story involving big terms like cellular respiration and anaerobic fermentation, but basically mitochondria are handy little grains that help turn oxygen into energy.

"To be a good long distance runner, you want to have sustainable energy," Alex Hutchinson told me, "that squeezes the most energy out of every bite of pasta that you eat and provides it in a way that doesn't cause you to feel tired prematurely. The mitochondria are what help you produce this aerobic energy that's long-lasting and efficient."

To get into Boston, then, I needed to get myself some more and better mitochondria. And in simple terms, the best way to increase the volume and effectiveness of your mitochondria is to run more. When you do more training, your muscles get more of these microscopic powerhouses, and each unit of them starts to work more efficiently and provide more energy.

Bring on the mitochondria, then. Bring on the training.

# CHAPTER 24

In *The LEGO Movie* (which I could almost recite from memory, my son and I have watched it so many times), one of the characters is a 1980s astronaut named Benny. No matter what the problem, Benny's proposed solution is to build a spaceship.

"Spaceship!" he shouts when he finally gets to do his thing. "Spaceship! Spaceship! Spaceship!"

For me, the word is not "spaceship" but "spreadsheet."

There are few important things in my life for which I have not set up a corresponding Microsoft Excel document. I can't help it; it's just the way I am.

There's a spreadsheet, not surprisingly, for my family's finances. There's one that analyzes the various ways I can use my credit card reward points so I can get the most value. When my family is approaching a busy weekend, I usually create a spreadsheet that shows what each of us will be doing at each interval of the day.

There's one that keeps track of all of my son's LEGO sets (name, product line, product number, how many pieces). When I'm curious about how the nutritional values of some of my favorite foods compare, I dump them all into a spreadsheet. If I'm watching tennis on television and I start to wonder what the odds are of Novak Djokovic equaling Roger Federer's record for career Grand Slam victories, based on how many each had won at various ages and stages of their career, then spreadsheet! Spreadsheet! Spreadsheet!

There's even a spreadsheet for this book. At the end of every day I spent writing, I updated a document that tracked how many total words I'd written and how close I was to meeting the milestones I'd set on my timetable.

So it's not surprising there's a spreadsheet on which I keep track of all the different aspects of my training. I count mileage. I record races. I document split times. I measure myself against the field, my gender, my age group. In what percentile did I finish? How does that compare to my last race? Where would I have finished if I had done the same race the previous year?

I run, and then I run numbers. I use online calculators to determine equivalent times among various ages and races. If I could run a 3:27:12 at age forty-four, what would my time have been at twenty-nine? What will it be at fifty-four?

I plan my races. What are all the different ways I can hit a 3:23:30 finishing time? How fast do I need to go in the first half – without going too fast, mind you, since I've made that mistake before – if I want to leave myself a minute or two of breathing room in the second half? What's the typical trajectory of my previous marathons – how much do I usually slow down after twenty miles?

This obsession with details, lists and data manifested itself in another way on my journey toward Boston: finding the perfect qualifying marathon to run.

Some component of this was just my normal compulsiveness, I grant you. But I could justify my quest to find the right course and the right timing with a number of excuses. First, based on everything I knew, I wasn't going to blow past my Boston qualifying time with twenty minutes to spare, so I needed every possible advantage working in my favor. Second, there are a lot of factors you can't control in a marathon, so why not do everything you can to influence those that are within your domain? And third, you can't run a marathon every few weeks. Realistically, you can take two or three shots a year at running a good long-distance race. And that's if you're healthy and can afford the time to train and race. So, you have to do everything within your power to make sure that when you do run, you have the best chance of succeeding.

There's an elaborate effort now underway to create the ideal conditions for someone to break two hours in the marathon in the next few years. For that to happen – for several minutes to be shaved off the current record – almost every possible factor must be controlled. You need the absolute best weather, from temperature to wind speed to humidity. You must find the best possible course: flat, maybe below sea level. The athletes must train in ideal conditions. They must wear the lightest possible shoes, or perhaps no shoes at all. Nutrition. Competition. Pacing. Genetics. The list of factors is endless. The organizers of this effort are trying to find ways to control every one of them – even delay the race by a day or two if the weather doesn't cooperate, maybe even change the course depending on the wind – in order to create the highest possible chance of success.

When Charles Lindbergh was preparing to fly the *Spirit of St. Louis* across the Atlantic Ocean, he disposed of the radio and trimmed the edges of his charts and maps to save weight. When your margin of error is small, you look for every tiny advantage.

That's how I approached my race. I was going to do everything I could to make my body stronger and faster, but I was also going to figure out exactly where and when I could give it the best chance of going as quickly as possible. So I began searching and scouring the Internet and every other reliable source of information to find the ideal location for my next qualifying race.

I couldn't control as many factors as a program with the quest of breaking the world record and a hugely symbolic time threshold equivalent to the four-minute mile. To qualify for Boston, you can't just wait for the ideal conditions and then go out and run twenty-six miles and three-hundred and eighty-five yards and send them your time. It has to be in a certified race, and those events don't adjust their date and direction based on the weather just to give you a little bit of an extra advantage.

But I could look at a wide range of variables in choosing the right race: time of year, weather, type of course, number of participants. There are marathons that bill themselves as flat and fast. There are downhill races. While no one can control the weather, there are marathons that are run at typically cool but pleasant times of year. And there are smaller events, even those that promise a cap on participants, so you aren't stuck behind a huge crowd of runners and unable to navigate the course quickly.

Beyond the websites and brochures of the marathons themselves, there are countless other resources available to the curious modern runner. Once upon a time, runners relied mostly on word-of-mouth. But today, there are online reviews written by other participants. There's a website that lists the races with the highest number and the highest percentage of Boston qualifiers each year going back to 2003. It doesn't compare the results from year to year, but once you dump the data into a spreadsheet, you can do that yourself!

There's another site that uses a complex formula to create equivalent times from race to race and year to year, based on factors like the kind of course and the weather conditions on specific race days. If you enter your race time from the 2006 New York Marathon, for example, it will tell you what an equivalent time was for the Big Sur Marathon in 2010. I have no idea how reliable it is, but it was a nice little outlet for my compulsive urges.

Let's just say I got to know these and other websites quite well.

I started to establish some rough criteria. Ideally, I wanted a race that was within driving distance, meaning somewhere in the northeastern U.S. or central Canada. I don't perform well in hot weather, so I needed a race in early spring or late fall, with a relatively early start time to reduce the risk of running the crucial last few miles under the midday sun. When you start to become knowledgeable about the historical temperature and humidity for the third weekend in May in Kingfield, Maine, you know you're getting a bit obsessive.

Once upon a time, Boston insisted that qualifying races had to be loop courses, with the finish line within a few hundred yards of the start, so that the net altitude change of the race was close to zero. But then they started allowing point-to-point races, meaning a downhill course was an option. You can debate whether that's fair or not, but if you're going to give me the option of running a course with an inherent advantage, I'm going to take it.

To make things more complicated, I host a weekly television show on Sunday mornings, the point in the week at which most marathons are being staged. It's not impossible for me to miss a show once in a while, but it costs me money to do so. Ideally, then, I wanted to find a marathon that met all of my other criteria and also fell on a holiday weekend when perhaps we wouldn't be doing the show. Not that I was asking much of the marathon gods.

A typical training run with Bob included the latest information each of us had gathered on prospective races.

"There's a marathon in Cleveland," I might say. "It's about an eight-hour drive for us. But it's listed in an article I found as being one of the faster races, for whatever that's worth.

"Then there's Grandma's Marathon in Duluth, Minnesota. It's supposed to be a good race and a fast course, but it's not driving distance. There's another one in Oregon in early June that was recommended by *Runner's World*, but that's definitely not drivable. I found another race that's twenty-ninth on the list of Boston qualifiers, but only eight of the top thirty are in the first half of the year, so it's one of the best among that group."

What can I say? It helped to pass the time on a twenty-mile training run.

This wasn't a new field of discussion. When Bob had run his first successful qualifying race, we had registered for an October event in upstate New York. It was billed as a fast course, and appeared frequently on the various lists and charts we had consulted. As the date started getting closer, however, the forecast started predicting unusually hot autumn weather. For two weeks leading up to the race, we debated back and forth whether to travel to the race or stay home and run a nearby event on the same weekend. The local course was not as favorable, and it started an hour later, but the temperature was slightly better, and eliminating travel was also a consideration. Sometimes it's an advantage to wake up in your own bed. In the end, after much debate, we went with the closer race and Bob qualified.

By now, we were used to these kinds of deliberations. In early 2013, Bob and I discovered the Poconos Run for the Red Marathon in Pennsylvania. Like most people, I had heard of the Poconos mostly for its heart-shaped beds, but apparently there was a decent marathon there, on a course that declined several hundred feet from start to finish. We examined the course profile and the weather history. The race happened to fall on a long weekend when I was off work, so it seemed to be perfect. And a friend, the coach and prolific marathon runner Mark Sullivan, gave it his personal recommendation.

A few months before race day, however, the race website announced a big change. Because of construction, the course would have to change for that year. The net change in altitude remained about the same, but Instead of being mostly downhill with a few gentle rises along the way, the course profile was now a lot closer to being a roller coaster ride, with steeper declines and even a few big climbs.

Bob and I debated what to do for a few weeks. Eventually, without many other options and having already calibrated our training schedules to that weekend, we decided to go ahead. This would be my first serious attempt to get into Boston.

# CHAPTER 25

It's very hard to get to the finish line of a race if you can't find the starting line.

Bob and I are searching frantically for the Pocono Raceway, the famous NASCAR track in Long Pond, Pennsylvania, which is where the 2013 Poconos Run for the Red Marathon is supposed to start. It's where it will start, in about twenty minutes, whether we are there or not.

Considering it's a major landmark, it's surprisingly hard to locate, at least for two visitors on this Sunday morning in May. The minutes are ticking by and we can't seem to get my smart phone GPS to line up coherently with the streets we are traveling. According to my digital map, we drove past what should have been the entrance a couple of miles ago, but all we saw was an empty field.

We are not alone in this plight. There are other cars with runners inside them traveling through this residential neighborhood. Somehow, we manage to get in a row of vehicles that is traveling in the right direction and we find our way to the speedway.

It's a mad rush from the car to the starting line, but sometimes there is benefit to not having too much time to think about things.

It's barely a month after the bombings in Boston, so there is a tense and somber atmosphere, distinct from the start of any other marathon I've been to. Considering it's a small-town race with about six hundred runners, there is an overwhelming amount of security. The runners aren't being searched, but there is a clear show of force. Several military vehicles are parked at the start line and we are surrounded by about a dozen heavily armed police officers.

It's hard to imagine anything violent or insidious happening at an event like this, but why take any chances? Under the circumstances, a little overcompensation is to be forgiven.

After a heartfelt, proud rendition of the national anthem, in which almost all the runners participate, it's time to start the race. I'm hoping that the racetrack and the surrounding streets, like Andretti Road, are symbols of speed from which we can all take inspiration.

The course starts with the kind of gentle downhill we had all signed up for. But just over a mile into the race, we are climbing, about one hundred feet of elevation over the next mile. And six miles in, there begins a precipitous drop. In the space of just over two miles, we descend about two hundred feet. There are downhills that take the pressure off, that give you momentum and help you accelerate. And then there are those that punish you, leave you feeling like a runaway freight train careening out of control, wondering what damage you are doing to your legs. For part of this stretch, I feel like I'm hurtling forward, going faster than I would in a ten-kilometer race.

To make matters worse, it's warmer than I had hoped it would be. The ideal race temperature for me is about forty to forty-five degrees. Today, it's in the fifties and climbing, and there is some humidity in the air. Some parts of the course have a fine mist hanging in the air.

I finish the first half in 1:40:43, which translates into 3:21:38. If only a marathon were as simple as doing the second half as quickly as the first. In this case, I had no idea what the course had in store for me next. Just after the halfway point, there is a climb that feels like a steep set of stairs. In about half a mile, we ascend about one hundred and sixty feet. At twenty miles, I'm still on pace. My time translates to a 3:23:15. But I'm slowing down. Starting at twenty-one miles, my pace drops below my target. I run the final five miles at almost eight-and-a-half minutes per mile, almost a minute per mile slower than the first five miles.

In the end, the weather and the course conspire against me. I finish in 3:26:51. It's a personal best, but I am still almost two minutes away from Boston, not counting whatever extra time I'd need to ensure I made the cut. On the infield of the high-school track where the race finished was a high jump mat. I sat down there and waited for Bob to cross the finish line so I could give him my news.

On the original course, I likely would have made it. Because of the route change, I discovered later, the average finishing time was almost ten minutes slower than two years earlier, when not only the route but also the weather was ideal.

Any day you complete a marathon is a good day. And it's hard to be disappointed about finishing a marathon in my fastest time ever. It was still early enough in my quest for Boston that this race seemed like another important step forward. I wasn't discouraged, but I wasn't satisfied either. It's a long way to go to come up just short.

# CHAPTER 26

In my next attempt, I blew it. I admit it: I flubbed my line. I missed the championship putt. I served a double fault on match point. I had a flat tire on the way to the dream date.

As I approached my next marathon, in August 2013, everything was in place. I'd done all the training I needed to run a fast marathon, to finally break the barrier I'd chased for more than a year. I'd bumped up the volume of my training, to create more of those mitochondria. I had a solid plan for how I was going to run the race. I had a friend who was going to accompany me for the final twenty kilometers, to keep me on pace and encourage me to finish strong. I was back on the loop course where I'd run the breakthrough marathon that made me think Boston was possible.

And then I did the stupidest, most boneheaded thing possible. I made a rookie mistake in my eighteenth marathon: I started way too fast.

I fell into the classic trap, the one I've warned countless other runners about. After a week of tapering, my legs felt strong. When the race began, everyone around me was running quickly and I had no problem keeping up. Running on the course where I'd surprised myself a year earlier made me over-confident. I felt like I was about to destroy my record and earn a trip to Boston. I had too much energy and enthusiasm.

For a while, I didn't think I was going too fast. When I looked down at my watch and saw a surprisingly fast pace, I thought there was something wrong with the GPS. Sometimes it's not reliable in the first mile of a run and it gives me a false reading. I didn't feel like I was running as fast as my watch was telling me, so I just kept going.

I should have known better. I should have slowed down. I should have listened to the voice of doubt in my head instead of the foolish hope in my heart and the short-lived energy in my legs.

To get to my goal time, my average pace needed to be about seven minutes and forty-seven seconds a mile. It's okay to start a bit faster than that, but I ran the first loop of the course, about three miles and a quarter, almost thirty seconds per mile faster than my target. I was basically doing a marathon at my half-marathon pace.

I slowed down a bit over the next few laps, but by then it was probably too late. I crossed the halfway mark in 1:39:15, two-and-a-half minutes ahead of schedule. There's starting a little bit quick and having some time in the bank in case you slow down in the second half. And then there's running beyond your capacity and guaranteeing you'll run out of gas before the race is over.

To put it in perspective, that first half was only forty-nine seconds slower than my personal record for the half-marathon. I figured the odds were about ninety-five percent the whole thing was going to blow up in my face and I'd be walking the last few miles. Otherwise, I was going to have an amazing day. I clung to the hope of that five-per-cent chance for as long as I could. But I knew it was a longshot to run a near-record half-marathon and then another strong half-marathon immediately after that.

I ran the fifth of eight laps at exactly the pace I should have been running from the start. But it wasn't long before I was slowing down and losing energy. My friend Brent joined me in the second half of the race. He asked me how it was going and I told him my pace and my resulting fears. He did his best to keep me motivated, but the laws of physics are irrefutable.

For the next lap, I was over eight minutes a mile. Then eight-and-a-half. In the final lap, I passed a water station where another friend was volunteering. "You're looking strong," he said. I knew he was a Boston Red Sox fan. "I'm running like David Ortiz," I said, referring to the slugger known for his power and not his speed. I felt like I was rowing across a lake in a leaky rowboat, pumping the paddles furiously as the water built up around me.

Somewhere in that last lap, Brent tried to offer me some encouragement, pointing out I was completing my eighteenth marathon. "That's pretty impressive," he said. "Where will number nineteen be?" I remember thinking, *We know where it won't be: Boston.*

I finished in 3:30:50. Only a year earlier, that would have been my fastest marathon in four years and less than a minute short of my personal record. Instead, it was a huge disappointment. Both my wife and my training partner asked me why I'd gone out so fast. My only answer was that I couldn't help myself and that I'd been foolish.

My bad execution cost me a spot in the 2014 Boston Marathon. Like so many runners, I had wanted to run the first marathon after the bombings, to be part of the show of resilience. My imprudence prevented that. The registration would soon open and there was no time for me to run another qualifying race before then. My plans were going to be put off for at least another year.

In the days that followed, I pulled out the silver linings playbook. I figured it said something that what would once have been close to a record was now a major disappointment. If I could almost break three-and-a-half hours on a bad day, then maybe I could go five minutes faster if I ran the race properly.

But I was starting to think I couldn't do it alone. I was going to need some help.

# CHAPTER 27

In the early days of my running career, when I was also exploring triathlons and writing a weekly column about endurance sports in the daily newspaper where I worked, I trained with a coach named Rick Hellard. Rick is a competitive runner and triathlete who has won many events, flirted with 2:30 in the marathon and trained hundreds of athletes to complete an Ironman triathlon, run their first marathon or finish in a personal record at any distance.

From Rick I learned, and wrote, about speed work and tempo runs and hill training. He taught me how fast to go on my long runs. He showed me when to schedule another event – a B race – before my goal race. Together with his group of charges, I did a lot of workouts with Rick, on the track and on the bike.

Rick is warm and funny, but he's also one of the most competitive people I know. He expects a lot of both himself and his clients. In fact, I think he expects his clients to be just as intense as he is. On one weekday evening, a group of us was running a five-kilometer time trial. Rick came up behind two of us and barked, "If you can talk to each other, you're not running fast enough." When I competed in my first Olympic-distance triathlon, my primary goal was to finish. I trained with a friend who had the same objective, so we decided to stick together on race day. When we were completing the final loop of the run together, Rick passed us. He was doing an iron-distance event on the same course. "You guys should be racing *against* each other, not together," he shouted as he charged ahead of us.

When I was close to finishing my first book, I reached out to a few people for suggestions on a title. Rick wrote back with a few ideas. I replied to him, "I expected you to suggest *You're Not Going Fast Enough* as the ideal title.'" He said that was actually the headline of an article he'd written.

When my wife and I had children, I ran out of time to train for triathlons. I decided I didn't need a coach, but I stayed in touch with Rick, who was a valuable source of information for my columns and a reliable guest on my radio show. So after my disastrous result and second failed attempt at qualifying for Boston, I knew where to turn for help.

We met at a coffee shop about two weeks after my race. I told him about my foolish behavior in the first half of the marathon.

"Well, you won't make that mistake again," he said.

I do a bit of consulting work with small businesses, and I often tell prospective clients that no matter what your skillset, it's hard to be responsible for both planning and execution at the same time. You might possess the knowledge and ability to excel at either role, but it's unlikely you'll do both of them well. Someone needs to be the coach and someone else needs to be the player.

I'm also a strong believer in relying on people with expertise. Whatever you're going through, in life or in running, many other people have experienced it before. And still another person has worked with dozens of those people and has learned from all of those cases. Why fumble around as a rookie, wasting time learning lessons first-hand, when you can benefit from the knowledge of someone who has seen it all before?

Unless you have a lot of time on your hands, you can't be as good as someone who works full-time in the area where you're dabbling. Whether it's home improvement, financial planning, child psychology or marathon training, there are pros with whom you couldn't possibly keep pace in terms of the latest knowledge and expertise. So why bother trying?

When you have a coach, you put all of the decisions in another person's hands. Your job is to do what you're told and report back on the results. You also have someone who holds you accountable – perhaps someone who is even tougher than yourself – but also someone who will tell you when to take a day off. You have a source of feedback, someone who will tell you when you're on the right track.

Without a coach, a lot of runners resort to applying knowledge they pick up on the fly. They read an article or overhear another runner talking about a new training method. They change their tactics or their shoes or some other part of their training, sometimes very late in the process.

Reaching the next milestone in your running is not just a function of training harder, it's also about training smarter. A coach will prescribe workouts that you'd never do on your own. You'll have much more variety in your workouts, which means they are more likely to create a training benefit compared to repeating the same runs over and over again. And you're more likely to do those workouts if you're answering to a live human being rather than just trying to follow a training program from a book, when only you know whether you've done the workout or not.

With a coach, you'll not only be better prepared, you'll *feel* better prepared. You'll gain confidence from hearing someone tell you that they've seen other people do it before and get the results they wanted.

Not everyone likes a tough coach, but I prefer working with people who are hard to please. I like the threshold to be high. When Rick says I've done a good job, I know he's not just being polite.

Rick and I went over my recent training programs and race results. He said he thought I was close. I was ready to trust him with the job of figuring out how to close the gap. From now on, I would be accountable only for completing the runs he prescribed. My job was to do what I was told.

# CHAPTER 28

When I was training for my first marathon, I attended a talk by a coach and experienced long-distance runner. He told the audience, most of whom were rookies like me, that you didn't really know what you were doing until your tenth marathon. I remember thinking, "Ten marathons? I'm not even sure I can do one!"

There are a lot of variables to marathon training, and what's effective for another runner may not work for you. So there is a lot of trial-and-error to figuring out what works specifically for you, in your training and on race day. And even if you train full-time, you can't run a serious marathon every weekend. The people who do twenty marathons a year are not trying to do a personal best in any of them. Most runners can only attempt to train for and complete a fast marathon two or three times a year.

Even when you run a successful marathon, you may not be sure what factors contributed to it. Did going a little longer on your weekend runs help your cause? Were the new gels effective? Did the new lighter shoes make a difference? Or was it all because the weather was cool and you got a good night's sleep? You may never know.

By the time I was training with Rick again, I had completed eighteen marathons. But even though I was almost double the supposed threshold at which you started to figure things out, I still didn't know the best training plan for me. I was happy to have the input of a professional.

A few days after we met, Rick sent me a detailed spreadsheet with all of my workouts laid out until race day. It was an aggressive training program and it was exactly what I was looking for. If I had the time, I would train as often as an elite athlete to achieve this goal. So I was ready to stretch my limits.

The typical marathon program might build up to a couple of runs of nineteen or twenty miles, maybe slightly longer, three to six weeks before race day. Rick had me running nineteen miles or more about seven times, starting almost three months before the race. It might sound like a lot of mileage, and I wouldn't recommend it to a novice marathoner, but because I'd been training hard for a couple of years, the extra distance was a manageable jump for me.

But on some of those runs, I wouldn't just be putting in the miles at the traditional slow pace to build up endurance. Rick had me do at least a portion of many of those runs at my goal marathon pace or faster. The workouts looked something like this:

Run 25k (about 15.6 miles) as follows: 5k easy, 3x5k at marathon goal pace with two minutes' rest, 5k easy

Run 30k (about 19 miles), increasing pace every 10k

Run 30k, increasing pace every 5k

Run 35k (about 22 miles) with the last 5k at marathon goal pace or faster

Run 38k (about 24 miles) with the last 5k at marathon goal pace or faster

Considering most of my long runs in the past had been at a comfortable pace, many of these runs seemed daunting to me. Would I even be able to complete them? How painful and challenging would they be? What if I couldn't handle the speed and had to stop, miles from home?

When I trained on my own, my weekday runs were typically about forty-five minutes at a steady, fairly relaxed pace. Once in a while I might go a little faster or farther to test myself. Now, Rick wanted me to do some one-hour runs with a portion of the run at marathon or even half-marathon pace. On top of that, he also started me on interval workouts: five repeats of one-kilometer (about three-fifths of a mile), eight four-hundred-meter repeats, and so on.

If all of these runs didn't kill me, they wouldn't just make me stronger – they would improve my confidence a great deal. I knew that if I was going to be faster and tougher on race day, I needed to run harder and longer in my training. I wasn't sure how hard or how long I could go, but I decided the only thing to do was trust Rick and see what happened.

Along with trusting a coach and searching for the perfect race, I also made sure I had all the tools and support I needed to get the most out of my body. I started going for massages more often. I had some of my aches and pains treated by a specialist in active release technique, or ART. I bought a foam roller, a giant blue cylinder against which I would reel my body back and forth to stretch out some of my tender muscles.

Every week, I would send Rick a report and he would send me his feedback. It felt good to have not only his guidance, but his approval when I did well. In early November, I fired off a spreadsheet that showed that on my one-hour run, I had completed 12.97 kilometers (about 8.1 miles), 10k of which was at exactly the pace I would need on race day. I also did a thirty-kilometer long run, the middle third at marathon race pace and the final third at better than my half-marathon pace. I was starting to feel faster and more powerful, and my goal was starting to seem more achievable.

"That is an excellent week of running, capped off with a great 30k," Rick wrote back to me. "Keep up that kind of good work and you WILL get to Boston."

And then he added, "Oh, and 12.97k can be rounded up to 13k if you want."

What can I say? I like being precise.

As it turns out, I hit many of the training runs out of the park. I started doing the final segment of some of my long runs at a pace that was in between how fast I'd run a half-marathon and a 10k. For some of my long runs, I was finishing in roughly the time I would need to be at the same distance on race day. And the next day I wasn't completely exhausted or unable to move. I was starting to believe a faster marathon was very possible.

# CHAPTER 29

Friday the 13th of December, 2013 was ominous for more than just the superstitious. As I looked ahead to my weekend long run, the weather forecast seemed more frightening than unlucky.

With my confidence building, I no longer found the numbers in my training program daunting. But the weather was a different story. For Saturday morning, the meteorologists were calling for minus-eleven degrees Fahrenheit, but with the wind it was going to feel like minus-twenty-seven or worse. On Sunday, it was supposed to warm up to a balmy zero, but heavy snow was also coming, and the winds were expected to pick up to thirty miles an hour.

My choice, then, was to run on a clear but blistering cold day, or try my luck in a blizzard.

That's a familiar predicament for northern runners. But this was to be no ordinary run. Just two weeks ahead of my next marathon, I was supposed to cover twenty-four miles, including the last three at my expected race pace. This run was to be the pinnacle of a new program – supplied by my coach, Rick Hellard – that would take me farther and faster in my training runs than I'd ever traveled before.

I've run on colder days, but never for this long. So over the course of that Friday the 13th (in the last month of a year ending in 13, no less) I clicked on the weather forecast two or three times an hour, hoping to see some improvement on either day, something that would help me decide when would be best to brave the elements. Nothing changed.

Avoiding the weather was not an option. I occasionally run on a treadmill, but the most I can manage without succumbing to sheer boredom is about an hour. That was barely 30 percent of the time I needed to be moving.

And I'm too busy during the week to push my long run to

Monday. Maybe I'll be able to do that when I'm retired (although by then I hope to avoid winter weather by using travel rather than procrastination).

In the end I chose footing over temperature. For this important run, I figured I was better off being cold than sliding all over snowy sidewalks.

My training buddy Bob and I set out at 10:00 am on Saturday, both of us bundled in layers, he with plastic bags over his socks for wind protection.

For many of my long runs, I keep it simple: travel half the distance and then turn around and head home. But in these conditions, I didn't fancy running into the wind for twelve consecutive miles. So apart from one or two straight stretches, we ran a series of loops around different parts of our neighborhood, including an office park.

It wasn't the most exciting route, but it meant that we were never far from home in case something went wrong, and we were never running straight into the wind for longer than ten or fifteen minutes.

Bob was planning to join me for twelve miles, but I convinced him to do an extra one or two for moral support. That still left me with ten or eleven on my own. After dropping him off at his house, I headed straight into the squall so that I could finish with the wind at my back. That first solo stretch was the toughest of the day.

But even that wasn't as bad as I expected. And it certainly wasn't difficult finding the inspiration to speed up for the last three miles. After all, it meant the whole ordeal would be over sooner.

I felt prouder at the end of that run than I have at the finish line of some marathons. When I peeled off my clothing, I noticed one of my toes was sore and discolored, its nail purple. Fortunately, that turned out to be bruising and not frostbite.

I sent Rick a note. "Will send you the full update later, but I got it done," I wrote. "33k at 5:17, 5k at 4:45. F--- it was cold and windy, though."

Rick wrote back, "I have never heard you swear before. I am going to save this message. That is a very impressive run today (again). Two more weeks and we get to see what happens when it's actually a race day. Should be very exciting."

I had done everything Rick had asked me to. Now, apart from a few final, shorter runs over the following two weeks, there was nothing to do but get ready for the race.

When you start running, you think the training is just about preparing for your goal race. But it's worth so much more than the physical benefit. Many training runs are as challenging as the race itself. They are magnificent and memorable tests. And when you meet the challenge, you are emboldened, reinforced, validated. As a guy who despises cold weather and never thought of himself as tough, I find a brave winter run can be very empowering.

This frigid long run, though, was my final preparation for a race I was about to do in Florida, where the conditions were certain to be much different. Even in the northern part of the state, and at the coolest time of the year, there was no chance that race day would be a similar experience. Can a training run in early Canadian winter really prepare you for a race in tropical heat? Yes, in one important respect alone: once I finished that run, I thought I was ready for anything Florida could throw at me.

# CHAPTER 30

Two weeks after that bitterly cold, character-building run, and three days after Christmas, I was on a plane to Jacksonville.

This was going to be a quick trip. I would be in Florida for about thirty hours, at least eight of which I hoped to be sleeping and no more than three hours and twenty-four minutes of which I intended to be running. I packed incredibly light: I would wear almost exactly the same clothes on the flight home as on the journey to Jacksonville. I wore my running shoes on the plane and put all of my race-day gear in my briefcase with my laptop computer. A t-shirt, hat, shorts, socks and a few gels don't take up that much space.

I picked the Jacksonville Marathon because it was promoted as a very flat course with not even a bridge or an overpass on the route. As I discovered through my relentless and compulsive research, the race had regularly made it onto the list of top Boston-qualifying races. Although it wasn't ideal to leave my family over the Christmas holidays, it was a bit easier than squeezing it in around a busy week at work.

My training had gone extremely well. As I waited in the departure lounge, I pulled out my computer and looked back over all my training runs to see the results of Rick's good planning and my hard work. I was feeling very confident.

I was even somewhat optimistic about one factor I couldn't control: the weather. I had been tracking the forecast for weeks. On November 27, I emailed Bob with the exciting news that in northern Florida, it had actually dipped below the freezing point. "Today: Low 28, high 59. Really long-range forecast for December 29: Low 45, high 63. Cloudy." And then I added: "How they know anything about the weather a month in advance, I have no idea."

Perhaps it would have been better to question why I was even checking the forecast a month in advance.

A few days later, on December 1, I shared the race-day forecast with Bob once again. "Sunny, low 36, high 57. I would take that."

On December 13, just over two weeks from race day, I provided another update. "Current long-range forecast is cloudy, low 43, high 66."

Don't think I hadn't checked the forecast in the twelve intervening days, by the way. I just didn't share it with Bob.

One week later, another update: "Forecast for Jacksonville December 29: Cloudy, low 39, high 66."

When you're planning to run a morning marathon, the forecast low temperature is just as important as the high. If you're starting at 7:00 am, you likely won't still be running when the high temperature is reached in the middle of the afternoon or later. So even on a day when there's a warm high, you might be able to outrun most of the heat if the day starts off cool. I was certainly encouraged by those low lows.

As I suggested in my email, a long-range forecast isn't very reliable. The morning before the race, while I was actually on route to Jacksonville, I received an email from the race organizers. I discovered it while I was changing flights in Philadelphia.

"Dear Mark Sutcliffe," it read. "We wanted to give you the current weather forecast, as it has changed since our last email."

Uh-oh. "We will run the race in the rain and would delay the start of the race if lightning is in the area at the 7:00 am starting time."

Lightning? "The weather is going to be warm and humid. Be sure to hydrate before the race with water and electrolytes." After a few more logistical notes, the race ended with a cheerful, "Happy Running!"

The hour-by-hour forecast pasted into the message showed the temperature rising from sixty-nine at the start time to seventy-two by 11:00 am. The humidity was 93 percent. The winds were at twelve to fourteen miles per hour. And the forecast called for thunderstorms from 7:00 to 9:00 and scattered thunderstorms after that.

Happy running, indeed.

I arrived in Jacksonville and went straight to my hotel. I had nothing to do but eat and sleep before the next morning. The event was small enough that I could pick up my bib number an hour before the race. The hotel was located on a pretty major thoroughfare with very little in the way of sidewalks. Without a car, I had to walk on the grass to get to a nearby restaurant. Then I just hung out in my room and watched a couple of movies. As the parent of two children under five years old, I wasn't used to having so much free time.

When I arrived at the start line the next morning, it wasn't raining, but the atmosphere felt ominous. It was dark and overcast and the air was thick. The public-address announcer at the start line repeated a message every minute or two, telling runners that if we saw lightning, we should take shelter. If we chose to continue running, we did so at our own risk.

Just what you want to hear on the day you're supposed to run the fastest marathon of your life.

Minutes before the gun went off, I saw a lot of runners exchanging sheepish glances. *What can you do*, they seemed to be asking. *Here goes nothing.*

For 7:00 am, it was incredibly humid. Three miles into the race, my shirt was soaked, and it hadn't even started raining. I saw a lot of men running shirtless. I'm not sure when the rain started, but within a few minutes it was torrential. I couldn't have been more wet if I had fallen out of a boat. I didn't see any lightning, so I was never forced to decide whether to abort the race or risk carrying on. But it was the hardest rain in which I'd ever run. Not even that bitterly cold and windy run of two weeks earlier could have prepared me for this.

In some of the race photos I perused a few days later, you can see the water pelting down on runners, their feet splashing in puddles. There are spectators in windblown rain ponchos, God bless them.

Somewhere in the final five miles, the humidity started to catch up to me, and I knew I was losing speed. I had no idea what was happening to my soaking wet feet inside my running shoes. In the final few hundred yards of the race, the course crossed a field and then finished on a high school track. The field was a mess, with mud four or five inches deep. I splashed my way across it, hit the track and then ran as hard as I could to the finish.

I finished in a personal record of 3:25:22, just twenty-two seconds from my qualifying time, but I knew that I needed much more than that if I were actually to get into Boston. I was about two minutes off my goal. As I had said in Pennsylvania seven months earlier, on another day this might have worked out better.

I told myself I would not be disappointed with another personal record. I was the sixty-eighth person across the finish line, out of more than eight hundred runners. I was ninth out of eighty-three people in my age category. Those are pretty good results for a guy who's used to being in the middle of the pack. But they still weren't good enough.

As I took the shuttle bus back to the hotel, I remembered: I had brought only one pair of shoes and now I had worn them in the rain for hours. I used the hair dryer in my room for about thirty minutes on each shoe, but it was no use. They were still soaking wet when I got in a taxi to head to the airport. This was going to be an inglorious trip home.

# CHAPTER 31

When you come that close to your goal, when you improve over your previous time, when you know there are factors that worked against you, that cost you precious seconds and minutes, there is only one thing to do: plan another race and start all over again.

I briefly considered finding a race early in the new year, to take advantage of the fitness I had proven through my training runs and the somewhat encouraging but still disappointing result in Jacksonville. But I soon learned that the Poconos Marathon, held in the spring, was reverting to its original course, and Bob and I decided we had to give it another try.

Once again, I dove head-first into another cycle of training, of long-distance runs in which I accelerated beyond my marathon goal pace and weekday sessions that stretched the limits of my speed. I met every test that Coach Rick provided for me. I exceeded my own expectations. And despite how unfortunate my race day experiences made me feel, I had to consider myself lucky that I never got injured.

In May 2014, I was ready for another race. I made only one major change to my training plan: I asked Rick to move the last significant long run, of twenty-four miles, to three weeks before the race instead of two. I wanted to extend the tapering period, to make sure I was well-rested on race day.

So here we go again. The familiar cycle repeats: You say goodbye to your family and climb into a car on a Saturday morning. You think about the fact that the next time you see them, the marathon will be in the past. You will either be celebrating or telling them how, once more, you came up short. You drive five or six hours to a small town in Pennsylvania. You check into an old hotel in the center of town, where you ask the front desk manager for a quiet room because you need a good night's sleep before the marathon. "Good luck with that," he snorts. There's a wedding and a prom going on that night, he tells you. Nothing like good old-fashioned customer service.

You go to your room, unpack your bags and wash your face. When you gently pull on the towel by the sink to dry yourself, the rack comes off the wall. This is a reflection of the quality of the establishment, not your superhuman strength.

You head off to register for the race. You follow a tradition you've established of having an early pasta dinner at about 4:00 in the afternoon on the eve of the race. You and your training partner walk around the town looking for a restaurant that will serve supper that early and stumble upon a sports bar where you consume as much pasta and bread as you can. You drink a lot of water and head back to the hotel. You watch a bit of television together, maybe a ballgame or some playoff hockey. You figure out the final plan for the morning. You wish each other a good night and head to your respective rooms.

You lay out some of your clothes for the morning and you set your alarm. You try your best to get to sleep. You count the hours until the race will actually start. When it does, you tell yourself, you'll feel better. There will be nothing left to do but run.

You rise early and get dressed. You store your gels in every available pocket. You pin your bib number. You double-check and triple-check to make sure you haven't forgotten anything (there was that triathlon where you left your wetsuit hanging in the front hall). You close the door to your room. You think once again, *When I get back, it will be over, one way or the other*. You meet your partner and you drive to the start.

So much of the experience seemed familiar. But the morning of the race was cooler than the previous year. And this time Bob and I were able to find our way to the start line more easily, restored to its original location at a well-appointed high school in a place called Little Summit. The morning was much less eventful than the previous year. After discarding a few throwaway clothes, we were off.

The early part of the course featured a much more gradual but steady downhill. There were a few climbs but they were mercifully short. My main memory of the first half of the race was the 3:25 pace bunny drifting in and out of the picture. Even though my watch told me I was running a consistent pace, and that I was on course for something around 3:23, I could never seem to shake the guy. He and the runners following him would fall behind for a minute or two and then they would catch up, surrounding me and even getting a few paces ahead.

This game of leapfrog was particularly evident because the pace bunny was very chatty. So even when I couldn't see him, I could hear him, talking away to his charges. Some people find conversation a welcome distraction that helps pass the time, but I prefer a quiet race. A few words here and there are okay, but for me, this was a race, not a social event.

I'm not sure if the noise gave me extra motivation to leave him behind, but eventually I stopped hearing his voice. I maintained my pace for fifteen miles, then twenty, then twenty-two. It was beginning to seem achievable, but I never count on anything until I can see the finish line. A marathon is both a physical test and a mental battle. There is lots of time for self-doubt. A runner passes you and you wonder if you will catch him again. You feel twinges and pains here and there and wonder if they will develop into something serious and threatening. You feel the miles accumulate and speculate about what kind of toll they are taking.

You reassure yourself, over and over again, *This is what I prepared for. This is what I've proven I could do, in training and in some of the races where the conditions were stacked against me. This is exactly where I wanted to be at this point in the race. Just keep going.*

# CHAPTER 32

There is a part of the marathon of which I never speak to first-time participants. When fatigue and doubt begin conspiring to crush your dreams, usually some time after twenty miles, it takes every shred of energy and willpower to keep going. It can be dark and discouraging, but getting through it can be one of the most validating experiences of your life.

The first half or a marathon is usually very straightforward. You start the run with vitality and zeal, hope and buoyancy. Your feet and your mood are light. If you're running with others, you're probably pretty chatty in the early part of the race. Maybe that helps pass the time; maybe it's an outlet for some nervous energy.

If you're well-prepared and well-rested, it should be no problem to stay on pace through thirteen miles. The greatest risk, as I proved in one of my Boston-qualifying attempts, is not going too slow, but too fast. At the exact halfway point, it's tempting to ask the question, *Can I really do this all over again? I just ran one half-marathon; can I do a second right on its heels?* You can offer yourself a quick reassurance that this is precisely what you have trained for, but it's probably best to avoid thinking about it too much. The distance can be a bit mind-boggling.

In my experience, the second half of a routine training run usually goes by more quickly than the first. I'm sure there's a psychological explanation for that. Perhaps it's because each subsequent mile is a smaller percentage of the total run (like how the years fly by increasingly quickly as we age). There is evidence that the passage of time accelerates with familiarity, so if you turn around in the middle of a run, maybe it's logical that time moves more quickly the second time you travel the same ground. Whatever the reason, I find training runs are like vacations: it takes a while to get to the halfway point, but the next thing you know, you're almost home.

If only that were true of a marathon. For me, the next segment of the race does pass by fairly quickly. I find that unless something goes horribly wrong or there's a strong headwind, miles fourteen through eighteen pile up before you know it. If it's going well, your confidence grows, maybe even to a false level. You start to think you could run all day.

You are completely wrong, of course. Somewhere between nineteen and twenty-one miles, I start to get a little more focused and anxious. I know what lies ahead is the true test of the marathon. Everything else to this point has been merely the prelude.

And then come the gloomiest and most demanding steps of any run. Unless you are blessed with the race of your life, as you pass twenty-two and twenty-three miles, you slowly descend into the darkest and quietest period of the marathon. You notice every incline on the course. You become aware of all the parts of your body that are bearing the toll of the run. The miles seem to stretch on forever. You scan the horizon, hoping to see the next mile marker come into focus, like a mirage in the desert. When another runner passes you, it's hard not to take it personally, to see that runner as a version of what you could be, if only you had more ability or fortitude. You know that even though you were flying at eighteen miles, you could be walking in a hundred yards. You have no words to say to anyone.

This is where, at least for me, all the self-doubt of a lifetime surfaces. This part of the marathon is like a desperate, late hour of insomnia, when the resources you deploy to drive the voices of negativity and uncertainty from your mind are depleted. You can no longer hold back the waves of pessimism; they crash over the barricades and wash over you. The menu list of past failures appears before your eyes. The familiar taste of defeat and insecurity arises from the pit of your stomach.

Somewhere in this stretch, you pass the threshold at which your training usually stops. So this is the most unfamiliar territory, where, presumably, the seconds tick by more slowly than ever. Time is not flying because you are certainly not having fun. You are deep into the race, but still not close to the finish. It's too soon to say it's almost over. When someone shouts "You're almost there!" you want to snap back, "No, I'm not!"

If you had any sense of humor left at all, you might be reminded of the line from Woody Allen's *Love and Death:* "I shall walk through the valley of the shadow of death. In fact, now that I think of it, I shall run through the valley of the shadow of death, 'cause you get out of the valley quicker that way."

In truth, no matter how fast you may wish to run, this is the point in the marathon at which all you can think about is walking. This is where the race is won and lost. This is where the goal is met or missed. This is the part of the marathon you must soon forget, or you will never do this again.

This is the great mental challenge of the marathon: to rally your spirit and compel your feet forward. This is not about all the times you got picked last. This is not another setback, not yet. This is your chance to hit it out of the park, and it's still alive. You have come so far. This can still happen. Today. All you have to do is keep moving.

# CHAPTER 33

After outrunning some of my demons in the late stages of the Poconos Marathon, I passed twenty-four miles. I was still running as hard as I could, but it was beginning to feel like I was losing steam. The first spasms were hitting my muscles. Fatigue was creeping up on me, alongside some faster runners.

I knew I had a little bit of time in the bank. It wasn't much, and it could all be squandered in the space of a few hundred yards. But I still had a chance to meet my goal. There was a slight uphill before we turned onto the main street in Stroudsburg, the final stretch from which we would eventually turn off and find the finish line. A volunteer shouted, "This is the last hill. You're home free after this."

And then my legs started to spasm some more and the pace bunny shot by on my right. And that's how I found myself to be walking, less than a mile from the finish, with another disappointment at hand. How could I come this close and still not get it done? Could I really end up running a great race for twenty-five miles and still not get the time I wanted?

After four or five steps, I decided I had come too far to stop without one last push. I repeated to myself a white lie I told myself in my very first marathon: *You only have to do this once.* Somehow, I started running again. If I stayed close enough behind the pace bunny, I figured, maybe I could put on a big surge in the final few hundred yards and catch him. Maybe I could squeeze out a 3:24:59. It probably wouldn't be enough to meet the ultimate threshold to get into Boston, but it would be the first time that I actually made my qualifying time.

I continued to run toward the school where the race finished. As I approached the road into the parking lot, I glanced at my watch. It read 3:17, which was a lot earlier than expected. And then I saw the 3:25 pace bunny ahead of me. He had stopped completely and was standing at the side of the road, holding his sign. Had he already finished the race? Was he waiting for someone?

I ran past him. As I entered the stadium, with about three hundred yards to go, I glanced at the clock at the finish line. It said 3:22. I still had a chance! I pushed as hard as I could for the final circuit and finished in 3:23:36. Only six minutes earlier I thought I had no chance. But now I had done it. In my twentieth marathon, I had finally finished in a Boston-qualifying time. And I had come very close to my goal of beating my time by at least a minute-and-a-half, to give me some breathing room for the final cut.

I walked slowly around the infield of the high school track, exchanging congratulations with other finishers and watching as more runners entered the stadium. Within a few minutes, I found the 3:25 pace bunny. "What happened?" I asked him. He told me he had become confused because there had been no sign indicating twenty-five miles. He thought he had fallen far behind his prescribed pace, so he sped up. Then when he arrived at the school, he realized he was way ahead, so he stopped.

Before the race, I had thought about the four potential outcomes for Bob and me on this day. It was possible that neither of us would qualify, just like last year. There was also a chance that I would make it and he wouldn't, or vice versa. And of course, there was a chance that both of us would hit our target and we could go to Boston together.

Of these possible scenarios, the worst, obviously, was for neither of us to make it. That wasn't going to happen now. The second-worst result would be Bob qualifying and me failing to do so. That was for practical, not selfish, reasons: Bob had already been to Boston and his qualifying time was more within his reach. It was more realistic, then, for Bob to qualify in a future race. Now I didn't have to worry about that outcome either.

So which of the two remaining options would it be? Ten minutes later, I got my answer. Wearing a bright yellow shirt, Bob came bounding into the stadium well ahead of his qualifying time. A year earlier, I had waited for him to arrive with a disappointed look on my face. Today, standing at the edge of the track before he began that final lap, I threw my arms in the air and shouted to him, "We did it!"

Bob told me later his watch had stopped working, so he was just running as hard as he could. It wasn't until I told him that he knew for sure he was on pace. He completed the final few hundred yards around the track and crossed the finish line with three minutes to spare.

For once, everything had worked in our favor. There was no construction, no weather system, no human error that got in our way. The one result we had been talking about for years had actually happened. We had both qualified for the Boston Marathon on the same day. Finally.

# CHAPTER 34

Bob and I made the long walk back to our hotel, basking in some combination of pain, joy, relief and maybe even a little disbelief. It was by far our slowest mile of the day – perhaps even the entire year – but it was certainly the most enjoyable. I was sore and weakened. My legs were fragile, and there were sensitive areas all over my body. Every step was now an adventure. But I was also walking on air.

In a few months, we would go online and register and then we'd wait to find out if we had made the callous-but-judicious Boston cut. For now, I wasn't going to worry about whether or not a minute and twenty-four seconds was enough of a buffer to get me in. For the first time ever I had beaten my Boston qualifying time. As far as I was concerned, I had made it to Boston. I had done my part; I'd leave the rest to some combination of fate and math.

The route back to the hotel was alongside the final mile of the race. We did our best to shout encouragement to the runners who were still on the course.

Once I was back at my computer, I finally got to write the email I had wanted to from so many hotel rooms on so many previous road trips. I hit reply on my wife's message from the night before, in which she had wished me luck.

"3:23:36," I wrote. "Finally. Bob qualified too. It was hard, and it warmed up more than I expected. But I finally did it, after twenty marathons. I've been waiting for this moment for a long time."

"Did you cry just a bit?" Ginny wrote back. "A little," I replied.

There is enormous gratification in the unambiguous result of a goal definitively achieved. So much of life is complex and nuanced and grey, but a finish line and a clock provide unmistakably clear answers. Just one of these rare, exquisite moments can make up for countless setbacks. In a lifetime spent coping with flashes of insecurity and anxiety, three of the most powerful words that can echo through your mind are *I did it.*

I sent my finishing time to my coach as well. "I hope that's enough to get me into Boston. Thanks for everything, Rick. All those great runs finally paid off. I'm thrilled."

A friend sent me a note. "How did the race go?" "Great!" I answered. "As in, Boston great?" she asked. "Yes!"

Many people assume the two things you look forward to most after a marathon, having sweated so much and burned so many calories, are a shower and a hot meal. But pouring water over your body after it's been exposed to almost three-and-a-half hours of repetitive motion is not a pleasant experience. All the sensitive areas of your body sting and scream. The shower is an ordeal, not a comfort.

As for food, during the week before a race, when I'm particularly careful about what I eat, I often envision what I will devour once I'm allowed to let loose and indulge. A celebratory meal is something to look forward to in the final hours of training. But I'm never actually very hungry after a race. There's some evidence that extreme exercise suppresses your appetite. You've been through such an ordeal that your body is more concerned about rest and recovery than food.

After checking out of the hotel, Bob and I boarded the shuttle bus back to the start line, where we had left Bob's vehicle, and began the long drive home. I don't remember much of what we talked about on the five-hour drive, but I'm sure we replayed the race over and over again. We also reminded ourselves to reserve hotel rooms in Boston the following April; if we waited too long, the best locations would be fully booked.

We did stop at a fast-food restaurant just off the highway. We hobbled into the restaurant, and for the first time in a few months I didn't think about how many calories I would be ingesting. I ordered a burger, fries, and a coke.

And then, after a few more hours of driving, it was time for another finish line: pulling up to my house at the end of a long journey, a trip that stretched back not just the hundreds of miles from Stroudsburg to home, not just the twenty-six fateful miles before that, but a quest that began years earlier, through thousands of miles of training runs and trips to other marathons. I was returning home to my family with my goal in hand. It wasn't a prize they could eat or take to the bank or hang on the wall, but they could celebrate it with me and know that my longtime obsession was almost over.

## PART 5

# THERE BUT FOR TWENTY-TWO SECONDS...

*"I'm at an ordinary – or perhaps more like mediocre – level. But that's not the point. The point is whether or not I improved over yesterday. In long-distance running the only opponent you have to beat is yourself, the way you used to be."*

**HARUKI MURAKAMI**

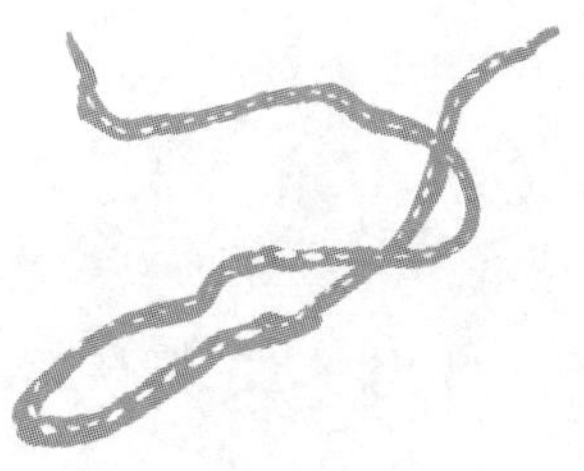

# CHAPTER 35

The email arrived at 2:37 p.m. on Wednesday, September 24, 2014.

The subject line sort of gave it away: "2015 Boston Marathon Confirmation of Entry Acceptance."

"Dear Mark Sutcliffe," the note began. "This is to notify you that your entry into the 119th Boston Marathon on Monday, April 20, 2015 has been accepted, provided that the information you submitted is accurate."

*Your entry:* bolded.

*Has been accepted:* bolded.

The organizers of the Boston Marathon certainly are aware of which five words are the most important to the recipient of such an email. Just so we are clear, it's *your* entry we're talking about, not someone else's. And yes, *you've* been accepted. *You're* in. If you read nothing else, read these five words. Don't just read them – absorb them, live them, celebrate them.

*Your entry…has been accepted.*

The email was actually much more detailed than that, some 300 words long. There was lots of information about logistics: registration, bib numbers, travel arrangements, hotels, blah, blah, blah. I didn't read any of it until later. Just that first sentence.

When you picture yourself being given the chance to fulfill a dream, you don't necessarily imagine the dramatic moment being when you receive an email. You're not thinking it will happen while you are checking your smart phone at work. But here was the final verdict on what would likely be my greatest accomplishment as a runner, arriving as a simple electronic message. In another time, presumably, it would have come not to my virtual mailbox, but to the old-fashioned one affixed to the outer wall of my home.

In fact, as I later discovered in the part of the email I hadn't yet read, a confirmation card would be sent to me through the regular mail within a few weeks. I was also told I could verify my acceptance to the field by searching the entrants' database on the Boston Athletic Association website, something I did more than once later that day and in the weeks ahead.

At exactly 2:38 p.m., one minute later, I forwarded the email to Bob. "I'm IN!!!!!!!!!!!!!!!!!!"

Now, as a writer, I almost never use exclamation marks. I think they're lame. My professional view is that if you have to use punctuation to put emphasis on something or tell the reader an exciting event just happened, you didn't do a good enough job with the words.

I made an exception here. In fact, I made eighteen exceptions here.

Since Bob had exceeded his qualifying time by an even bigger margin than I, it was certain that he had also been accepted. The following April, at long last, we would both be running the Boston Marathon.

# CHAPTER 36

So it came down to twenty-two seconds.

Something the confirmation email didn't tell me, but I soon found out, was that to be accepted into the 2015 Boston Marathon, you had to exceed your qualifying time by one minute and two seconds. I had surpassed it by a minute and twenty-four seconds.

I made it by twenty-two seconds. The length of a coughing fit or a voicemail message. The time it takes to warm up a coffee in the microwave. Or pay a bill online. Or tell a joke. An elevator ride to the tenth floor. Less than the length of a typical television commercial.

Less than one second per mile.

I ran for twelve thousand, two hundred and sixteen seconds. My margin of error for qualifying for Boston came down to less than two-tenths of a percentage point: 0.18 percent, to be exact.

If the Boston qualifying cut-off was a runner on the course, I could have looked over my shoulder and seen him chasing me, about eighty-three yards behind me when I crossed the finish line.

I went back to the results of my qualifying race, the Poconos Marathon. I was the last of eleven men in my age group to make it that day. Less than a minute behind me, there was a guy who had technically qualified for Boston, but missed the cut by thirty-one seconds.

In the 2013 New York City Marathon, there were 391 men in my age group who qualified for Boston, including fifteen who finished in the twenty-two seconds between me and the cut-off. One guy ran exactly the time that ended up being the requirement: 3:23:58. (I looked him up: he ended up running Boston much faster than that, so he certainly belonged there.)

Think about it: If I'd stopped to tie my shoe. If I'd stumbled in a water station. If I'd simply taken one second longer to run each mile.

Good thing I walked for only four or five seconds when the pace bunny passed me, and not thirty. If I had, the email I received from Boston would have looked very different. My face when I opened it would have looked very different.

"Thank you for submitting your application for entry into the 2015 Boston Marathon," it would have said. "Regrettably, we are unable to accept your application due to field size limitations and the large number of applications we received from those runners who met the qualifying standards."

Through social media, I found a guy who had missed by exactly one second. His marathon time was 3:28:59. The note read: "Entries from applicants in your age group were accepted through and including the time 3:28:58."

Ouch. A single second. And yet there must have been a few dozen runners like him. How many more were there between 22 seconds and zero? It's not a lot of time, but at the finish line of a big marathon, there may be five people crossing every second.

One second. No matter how much you're hurting in the final mile, you can always squeeze out another second. But not if you don't know you need to.

To make matters worse, the runner I found had missed Boston by two seconds the year before. I suppose he could reassure himself that he was getting closer.

According to Boston Marathon officials, a total of 1,947 runners who made their qualifying times didn't get into the race. It was even tougher the following year. To make it into the 2016 Boston Marathon, you had to exceed your time standard by two minutes and twenty-eight seconds. That means 4,562 runners who made their qualifying times were not allowed into the race. There are very few marathons that even have 4,562 participants. The Boston Marathon turns away that many who are actually eligible to run. I would have been one of them, if I'd run my qualifying time a year later.

(Here's an idea: if there are going to be thousands of runners each year who qualify but don't make the final requirement, there should be a separate race for them: the qualified-but-cut marathon.)

To qualify and not be accepted might be tougher to swallow than not qualifying at all. It's a long way to go, and I don't just mean the twenty-six miles on race day, to find out your qualifying time isn't good enough.

How many more people will be on the outside looking in next time? How much longer will demand continue to increase? How long will it be before they increase the standards again? By the time I reach my next age group, when I'm supposed to get another five minutes of breathing room, will I actually have to run just as fast as I do now to get in?

That's a problem for another time, because somehow I managed to make the cut. But if there are people on the outside looking in, with their noses pressed to the glass, wondering why they're not one of the lucky souls who got through the gate, I'm not going to look away. I'm on the inside looking out, but I'm sparing a thought for the people who got the unwelcome news, thinking, *There but for twenty-two seconds go I.*

# CHAPTER 37

Think for a moment about those 1,947 runners who qualified for Boston but weren't allowed in, including some who missed by a mere second. Isn't time cruel? It is heartless. It is unforgiving.

Time does not bend. It does not make exceptions. It does not hesitate.

No matter what they say, time is never really on your side. In fact, time doesn't choose sides at all. It has no favorites, shows no bias. It measures all, but works for no one. If you can't keep up, it does not flinch. It does not show mercy. It simply leaves you behind.

Time itself is infinite, but it is simultaneously the scarcest and most precious resource we know. It cannot be stored or saved. A clock may stop or malfunction, but time can never be suspended. You may feel sometimes like you're stuck on fast-forward, but there is no pause button and certainly no rewind.

And no matter what the self-help gurus say, time cannot be managed. You may learn to organize yourself around time, but you can never be its boss. You can't control it, handle it, command it or tame it.

Once lost, time can never be recovered. When you are stuck in a pointless meeting, when you listen to a relative describe a medical procedure in excruciating detail, when you are forced to spend ten minutes in a port-a-potty in the middle of the 2006 New York City Marathon, that time cannot be reclaimed. There is no appeal process, no return desk to visit to ask for it back. When you arrive five minutes after the train has left the platform, after the bank has closed, after the child's piano recital has ended, time gives no second chances. There is no undo button.

On a long and winding marathon course, there will be uphills and downhills. A headwind may become a tailwind. But time moves in only one direction: against you.

It's something you discover quickly in the role of pace bunny. When you maintain a specific pace with a group of runners in tow, when you carry a sign with a projected finish, you are the personification of time. You portray time in motion, for participants and spectators alike. If you stay on track, you move across the course like the hands on a clock, establishing a moving target for runners with a predetermined objective.

But your job is to be just as exacting as time. No matter how much it tugs at the heart to watch a runner fall behind, no matter how much you might like to reach back and collect her, to pull her along and help her catch up, you can't. You must represent not just the hours, minutes and seconds, but the simple, cold, harsh reality of time.

There are only two ways to measure a run: distance and time. One of these you earn, you acquire, you collect. The other you battle, you squander, you relinquish. The yards pile up, but the seconds slip away. The distance is manageable. It's the time that's in question. The miles will wait for you. The clock will not.

When a specific result is the objective of a run, whether that's a Boston-qualifying marathon, a quick 10k, or any other milestone, it is time and not any other runner that is your main opponent. Time is not only your goal but your ultimate archrival. It is the worst of all running partners. It is the most selfish of all companions. It charges ahead, with or without you. Time has only one job, to carry on a steady drumbeat, to mark the difference between yes and no, in and out, done or not done.

There are no timeouts in marathons. Once the clock starts, it can't be stopped for any reason. And you run every race like a team that is fighting from behind, the clock ticking down against you. As a runner, you never get to feel like someone with a big lead, who can simply let the clock run out to get the win.

On the right day, if you maintain the right pace, time cannot accelerate and chase you down. If you sustain the right speed, if you don't stop and let it catch you, time has no way to overtake you.

Time will run on, but at the finish line of a race, you get to stop the clock.

Time will be at the finish line in three hours, in four hours, in five hours, and every second in between. Time will be there when you are supposed to be. The only question is: Will you?

# CHAPTER 38

Time can boggle the mind. At the Berlin Marathon in 2014, Dennis Kimetto of Kenya finished in 2:02:57. At the 2011 Boston Marathon, Geoffrey Mutai finished in 2:03:02. Both performances work out to about 4:42 per mile, or 2:55 per kilometer.

It would be a big stretch for me to run a single mile in less than six minutes, let alone under five. Kimetto ran twenty-six miles in a row at sub-five-minute pace, without stopping. Put that in the perspective of a typical mile race. More than six thousand runners competed in the Fifth Avenue Mile in New York City in 2015. Only ninety-seven of them finished in 4:42 or faster. So Kimetto would have finished in the top one hundred of that race and then kept going for another twenty-five miles.

You know those chess masters that play a dozen games at the same time? You could set up a series of twenty-six one mile races, each featuring a field of six thousand fresh runners, and Kimetto could finish in the top one hundred in all of them, without stopping in between.

The average marathon time for men in 2015, according to Running USA, was over four hours and twenty minutes. For women it was four hours and forty-five minutes. That means the majority of runners wouldn't have even hit the halfway point in the course when Kimetto was getting his medal. He had a shot at not just showering and eating lunch by the time most people finished, but checking out of his hotel and getting on an airplane as well. If he'd pulled out his iPad at the finish line, he could have binge-watched six episodes of *The Big Bang Theory* before the average many crossed the finish line (of course, I have no idea whether he's into that show or not).

To put it another way, if you set up a race between the average marathon runner and Kimetto, even if Kimetto waited until Mr.

Average was at the halfway point to start his race, he'd still win.

The average finishing time for men in the half-marathon in 2015 was two hours and four minutes. For women it was two hours and twenty-two minutes. So if you put Kimetto into a half-marathon race, he'd finish it twice before most of the runners got to the finish line. That's assuming he could get around the glut of runners in his path on the second loop.

At major events like the New York City Marathon, you see runners who try to keep up with the elite athletes at the start of the race, just to show off or have a bit of fun. They usually last a few dozen strides and then drop off. A small number last a bit longer. I've always wondered what kind of shape they're in for the rest of their races. If you sprint for a couple of hundred yards right off the start, how much do you have in your legs for the remaining twenty-six miles?

The pace of an elite marathoner is almost impossible for an ordinary runner to understand. They travel at almost thirteen miles an hour. That's faster than some treadmills will go. My pace for short bursts of interval training is about eight miles per hour. I've done some triathlons in which I've barely hit thirteen miles per hour on my bicycle. Of course, if I had a time machine that could take me back to 1896, I could keep up with the leaders for about a quarter of the first Olympic marathon, in which the winner finished in just under three hours. Elite times have come a long way since then.

In the early days of automobiles in Britain, the speed limit was ten miles per hour. After thirty years, they raised it to fourteen. Think about how long it takes you to commute to work. Unless you are able to avoid rush hour, there's a good chance that Kimetto – and dozens of other elite marathoners – could match your time on foot.

To flirt with the gods for just a few seconds, I decided I would do a little experiment. How far could I run at the pace of the fastest marathon runners in the world? Before my test, I guessed I might be able to run a couple of hundred yards, or less than one percent of a marathon, at world-record pace. I'll get my excuses out of the way right up front: I was in the middle of training for a marathon, so I was running almost every day and my legs were not entirely fresh. I had also played tennis that day. And I'm not exactly in the prime of youth. Do I need to keep going?

Okay. I warmed up for a couple of miles at my typical pace of more than eight minutes per mile. When I glanced at my watch it seemed unfathomable that I could increase my pace by more than three minutes per mile. I paused, reset my watch and then ran as fast as I could down a stretch of empty road. When I couldn't keep up the pace any longer, I stopped and looked at my watch. I had run about three hundred yards in about 5:45 per mile.

I was still moving at a minute per mile slower than the world record marathon pace. And I'd barely run two blocks. I tried again, hurtling as fast as I could down the road, my arms pumping fast, my breathing rapid. I stopped and checked my watch. I had run just over two hundred yards at 5:25 per mile, still forty seconds off the speed at which a very small number of humans can run for two hours.

One more try: I rested for a minute, then launched into the fastest sprint I could imagine. I figured if I didn't run as far, I could go a little faster. I honestly moved as fast as my legs could carry me. After about a hundred and thirty yards, less than a tenth of a mile, I stopped. My pace was 5:02. I didn't even break five minutes per mile in what was basically a hundred-yard dash and some people could do it for twenty-six miles. At just over five minutes a mile, someone (not me) could run a marathon in two hours and twelve minutes – an elite performance, but still nine minutes off the world record.

Here's an important point: I wasn't running a marathon. At the speed I failed to hit, elite athletes are relaxed and settled in for the long haul, whereas I was sprinting, feeling my lungs burn, hanging on for dear life. It's not that they can run farther than me at the same speed, but that we are participating in completely distinct events. Traveling a few hundred yards at the world-record marathon pace is like the difference between sharing a hug with someone and being married to them for twenty-five years. It's like going on a tour of the White House and thinking you understand what it's like to be president. It's like watching the trailer for a movie and debating its merits with a seasoned critic who actually watched the film.

There are many parts of training and racing that are shared by amateur and elite athletes. No matter how fast or slow we run, we all know the commitment a marathon requires, what it's like to feel butterflies on the starting line, how hard those final few miles can be. But one thing that separates us is speed. The vast majority of runners will simply never know what it feels like to travel that fast.

PART 6

# GO, RANDOM STRANGER!

*"There are no standards and no possible victories except the joy you are living while dancing your run. You are not running for some future reward. The real reward is now!"*

**FRED ROHE**

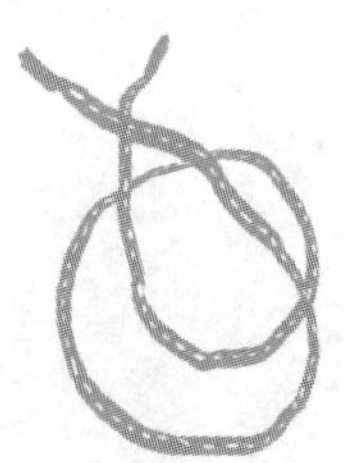

# CHAPTER 39

When I'm walking through the crowded departure area of a major airport, I always find it remarkable that all the people who are there will be somewhere else tomorrow. At this moment, we're all sharing the same space; within hours, we'll be distributed all over the world.

The travelers are carefully sorted by destination; each gate you pass is surrounded by a small population of people, all of whom are heading in the same direction. At Gate 19 is a group destined for Philadelphia. At Gate 20, the Miami-bound. Next are the people who will sleep in New York tonight.

In any departure lounge for Boston on Patriots' Day weekend, there will be a common purpose among many of the travelers. It's not hard to pick out the runners. Some are wearing Boston race jackets from previous years, others t-shirts from other marathons. Adhering to the rule that you should never risk losing your race-day footwear by putting it in a checked bag, some are wearing their running shoes; others have attached them by the shoelaces to their carry-on items. I haven't even boarded my flight and it feels like I already have one foot in Boston.

For this trip, my wife and I have left our children with their grandparents. So it's both a destination race and a getaway, an escape from the responsibilities of parenthood. Traveling without two toddlers in tow is an astonishingly liberating experience. I have to remind myself that I don't need to trade off with my wife if one of us wants to browse the magazine rack or go to the washroom.

We land in Boston and take rapid transit to the hotel. This includes a journey on the Green Line, the subway under construction at the time of the first Boston Marathon. It's immediately evident that it's the oldest subway in America; the cars and stations feel like a trip through time. The city is ready for the thousands of visiting runners; there isn't a single hospitality worker who doesn't know why we are here. Everywhere you go, there are words of encouragement.

The next morning, we walk to the finish line. It's looks much different from the last time I was here, almost nine years earlier, when I joined Dean Karnazes and the small group of runners for an unofficial run on the Boston Marathon course. Two days before the marathon, the street is already closed to traffic. Everything is in place, exactly as I have observed it countless times on television: the bleachers, the archway just beyond the finish, the large blue-and-yellow line.

In the windows of the Starbucks just yards from the finish are the words "You're almost there." They're meant for Monday's race, but they are just as appropriate today.

And everywhere, there are daffodils with the words "Boston Strong" on the flower pots. At the precise location of the first explosion in 2013, right across from the Boston Public Library, is a utility pole with crocheted flowers, ribbons, and pictures of the victims attached to it.

After an hour in a setting of so much triumph and tragedy, we meet up with my friend Bob and make our way to the race expo. The process is quick and efficient. Within minutes, we have our number bibs – mine is 12677. Bob and I pose for a picture in front of a giant wall of sponsor logos. A few yards away is an enormous poster in blue and yellow on which people are signing their names. I find one of the few remaining blank spaces and write the words "A dream come true" above my signature.

Just above my words is the signature of a woman from England. To the left is the name of someone from Spain. Just below someone has written, "Bucket list," with a checkmark next to it. Another message says, "Someday is today." There are hearts and happy faces. A woman has written, "My sister is here with me." It's not clear if she means that literally or figuratively.

Ginny and I meet a friend for lunch – a runner from Worcester, Massachusetts who has lived for years within a few miles of the start but this year will be running Boston for the first time. And then we walk to Fenway Park to take in a Red Sox game. It's cold and we are underdressed, which turns out to be a bit of a theme for the weekend:

that's how I'll feel at the start of the marathon.

On Sunday, Ginny goes for a run while I sit on a bench on Boston Common. I'm a big believer in tapering; I don't do anything at all for at least two to three days before a marathon. But others prefer to burn off some energy and keep their legs loose, even the day before the race. From my vantage point there are a lot of people running today. I'm sure they're not all spouses of race participants.

Finally, it's time for the pasta dinner. The mass gathering is held at Boston City Hall, a shining example of how brutalist architecture got its name. According to the *Boston Globe*, when the design was first unveiled to Boston Mayor John Collins in the 1960s, he gasped. Someone else blurted out, "What the hell is that?"

The building has been described as an upside-down wedding-cake. It's a structure made largely of concrete, and the interior seems no more welcoming and appealing than the exterior. It feels like it would be easy to get lost inside its bland corridors. In 2008, Boston City Hall was voted the ugliest building in the world in an online poll by a travel agency. Mayor Tom Menino reacted by saying the distinction would help draw tourists. Obviously he had a substantial silver linings playbook.

But I am here to eat, not to criticize the architecture. I have only a vague sense of – and huge respect for – the logistics involved in staging a major race. But the prospect of feeding tens of thousands of people in the space of a few hours seems even more daunting. The dinner is flawlessly executed, with hundreds of volunteers dishing out penne, rigatoni, meatballs and salad.

After we snake our way through the confusing floor plan, we find a place to sit. I'm not an expert on nutrition, so I have no idea if there are benefits to having pasta the night before a race. I do know that in 2008, I ran a particularly fast marathon the morning after a delicious restaurant meal of penne and tomato sauce, so on the eve of almost every major race since then, I've tried to replicate that experience. If nothing else, it feels right. And that's as important as anything the night before a marathon.

# CHAPTER 40

I would rather run than sleep. That's what my little obsession has come to. And although I can happily squeeze in a run at any time of day, my preference is always to do it first. There's something satisfying about starting your day with something hard, looking back throughout the day and knowing you ticked the box early.

At various times in my broadcasting career, I've worked an early-morning shift, so running first thing has not always been easy. But when I've had the chance, even when it's meant winding back the alarm clock an hour, I've often left my silent house under cover of darkness and headed out into the docile streets alone.

I remember one stretch during a recent autumn, when the windows in my schedule were closing more rapidly than those in my house. To make sure I didn't surrender a run to a busy workday, almost every morning I rose at 5:00 or 5:15, carefully dressed and tied my shoes in the blackness, and got out the door as quickly as possible.

I'm not immune to the temptation of a warm bed. And I crave and value my sleep. Look, I have multiple jobs and children. When I daydream about retiring early, I'm thinking about tumbling into bed at the end of the day, not finishing my career.

But I must have my runs. I know it's hyperbole, but I've convinced myself I can't function without them. Each night as I set the alarm, I reminded myself I would be weary either way. I could be tired and satisfied or tired and chagrined. I could be energized or sluggish. I could spend the whole day feeling like I was ahead, or like I was running – or not running – behind.

The first step of each run is always the hardest. At 5:00 a.m. that initial stride is the one made barefoot onto a cold floor. Once you have your running gear on, you have no choice but to go. And when you step out the door, your run becomes a fact. After a single yard, you've already gone too far to turn back.

On these early runs, the streets are quiet, but I'm not alone. There are, sporadically, people walking dogs or waiting for an early bus. Occasionally there is another runner. My usual route along an unlit path is not an option without daylight, so I run the busier streets of my neighborhood, though they are much quieter at this unearthly hour.

I pass by dormant shops and restaurants, darkened residential windows and empty cars. I time the glances at my watch to the passing streetlights. On some days, I run all the way downtown. Two hours later I'll be back, dressed differently and bemoaning the congestion. Now not only the sidewalks but the streets belong to me. I can run for ten minutes without seeing headlights.

At first it feels eerie, like a futuristic movie. After a few days, the familiarity becomes comforting. This has become my time of the day. When the weekend rolls around and I can run a bit later in the morning, it feels strange to see daylight. I have to remind myself to bring my sunglasses.

The temperature varies. Some early mornings are frosty, others still hinting at late summer. But it's cool enough that most days I wear gloves, just in case. The fingers are the first victims of the approaching chill. On one morning, a pelting rain tests my stubbornness.

But once the blood starts flowing more quickly, the feeling of satisfaction grows. And when I sneak back into the house before anyone else is awake, it feels like a minor triumph. I've claimed the last part of my day not surrendered to work and other evil forces. And I've disturbed no one. The benefits and consequences are mine and mine alone. I take off my shoes and wait for the rest of the house to come to life.

The energy will carry me through another long day. For a few weeks it becomes enough of a routine that on some days I even wake up before the alarm. I am craving the challenge, the solitude and the reward more than another hour of rest.

It's not something I'd do year-round – I like breaking up the day with a run, and I'd miss my running buddy – but sometimes, it's just as refreshing to change your routine as your route. Every run is a private and personal victory, and never more so than before the sun and your family arise.

On the morning of a marathon, you might rise just as early. You might still get dressed in the dark, put on the running shoes and head out of the door. But instead of being joined only by the shift workers and the early birds clutching their coffees as they shuffle to the bus stop, or walking their dogs before they head off to work, you are surrounded by activity. The hotel lobbies and streets are bustling. The coffee shops have opened early.

On the morning of a marathon, the streets are full of hope and anticipation. Nobody is sorry to be up early. Few of us would have slept much longer anyway, thanks to the anti-somnolent mix of anticipation and anxiety.

On the morning of the Boston Marathon, I met Bob, and together with our wives we walked from our hotels to Boston Common. The buses were lined up to take us to Hopkinton. We posed for a picture and we boarded with the other runners for the long trip that would remind us of how far we would be running back. The next time I saw Ginny would be just a few hundred yards from here, but on the other side of the journey I'd been waiting to travel for years.

# CHAPTER 41

Jerry Seinfeld once joked that based on the evidence, dogs are our masters and not the other way around. "If aliens are watching this," he said, "they're going to think the dogs are the leaders. If you see two life forms – one of them's making a poop, the other one's carrying it for him – who would *you* assume is in charge?"

Likewise, you have to wonder about how running a marathon would look to a visitor from another planet. Could you blame an outsider for thinking runners are the punished and not the privileged?

Think about it: You are awakened at an ungodly hour of the morning in an envelope of darkness. You leave behind the comfort of a warm bed. You dress quietly, solemnly attaching a multi-digit number to your chest and an electronic monitoring device to your shoe. You eat next to nothing. You trudge to a gathering place, often before the sun is even peeking over the horizon, wearing skimpy clothes and carrying limited provisions. You line up among thousands, all of you herded into a line that snakes toward a row of buses. As you board, you wave goodbye to your loved ones. You travel a great distance. You disembark in a tent village, where you sit wrapped in garbage bags and other disposable coverings, shivering in the cold and rain. You wait for hours. You seek the comfort and the company of strangers. And then, when the appointed hour arrives, you are marshalled through the streets, marching obediently into a gated corral. A gun is fired and you and all the others begin to run as fast as you can as bystanders scream at you from the sides of the streets. For the next few hours you sweat, you struggle, you expend all of your energy just to get back to the place where it all started in the wee hours of the morning.

What did you do to deserve this? Did you steal state secrets? Commit a series of violent crimes? Is this a code of justice from a science fiction movie brought forward to our time? Is it some perverse futuristic reality television show? No, you volunteered for this ordeal. You may have even traveled miles to do it, after preparing for months. You actually looked forward to it, couldn't wait for the day to arrive. You're not paying your debt to society, but you are paying cash for the honor and the pleasure of the experience.

Who would put themselves through this voluntarily? Even to someone from another place or period, it would seem perplexing. There are myriad reasons why we run, of course, but almost all of them are unique to our specific circumstances. Except for a few elite athletes for whom long-distance running is a profession, and a small number of others for whom it is a path out of poverty, the marathon is a modern, first-world phenomenon. In other places and at other times, no one has bought a gym membership or a pair of fancy running shoes, pursuing physical fitness in their spare time. Throughout history, most of the world's inhabitants have burned so many calories while at work that they neither need nor desire early morning hill workouts or weekend long runs.

What a luxury it is to have such personal goals, to be able to afford the time, the resources and the energy to strive for something beyond life's basic necessities, to have an arduous task on our bucket lists rather than our list of daily tasks. While life itself is a test of endurance for so many humans, as runners we seek out demanding challenges for the satisfaction of achieving something difficult. For many of us, the marathon is a way of afflicting our comfort and proving that despite our modern conveniences, we are worthy of the mantle that has been passed to us from previous generations whose struggle was so much greater than ours.

It is not exclusively for the privileged or comfortable, of course. There are thousands who run marathons every year despite illnesses and physical conditions or, indeed, because of them. For them, the marathon is an outlet, a cause, a demonstration that no matter what battles they face, they still have enough control over their lives and their bodies to get to a finish line far in the distance.

For most of us, though, running is a blessing and a validation. And so when you rise from that warm bed, when you line up for the bus, when you are transported that great distance and know you must run all the way back, when you crouch on the ground and shelter from the cold and rain and wait for it all to begin, there is no dread, only hope and anticipation. You relish the test, the chance to prove yourself. In an increasingly complex world, there is something deeply gratifying about doing something entirely on your own and literally one step at a time.

# CHAPTER 42

When I first started running, I thought of it as an individual sport. My early attempts at traveling a few miles felt protracted and lonely. Before long, however, I started training and talking with others and I quickly began to discover how genuinely welcoming and supportive a community is the nation of runners. Wally Herman, who has completed more than seven hundred marathons, once described to me the many wonderful souls he had run with by saying, "I never met a horse's ass in all those people."

Perhaps a big reason for the fellowship and camaraderie is the simple fact that while a marathon is a race, we aren't really competing with each other. So much of sports – indeed, so much of life – is a battle, a zero sum game. Only one team can win the World Series. Only one athlete can capture the title at the Masters or Wimbledon. Even at an amateur level, you and your friend can't both triumph in the game of squash or checkers or Monopoly that you play against each other. Only one candidate gets the job, only one family wins the bidding war for the house. Everyone can have a chance at the lottery, but there is only one winning ticket. Anyone can grow up to be president, in theory, but only one person in three hundred and fifty million can actually hold the job at one time. In so many elements of our daily life, success is absolutely finite. If you get it, I don't.

But with the extreme exception of the elite runners at the very front of the pack, in whose company most of us will never travel, and a small number of age-group athletes, everyone running a marathon can accomplish their goals on the very same day. Before other competitions, you can say "good luck" to another athlete in a gesture of sportsmanship. "May the best person win," you might even say. But in your heart, you know that one of you must fail, and you hope it's not you. In running, the many good wishes throughout your training and at the start line are genuine. There is no reason to hope that anyone else stumbles. There is no limit to the number of athletes who can run the race of their lives.

A thousand runners – or ten thousand – can achieve their personal best, all in the same race. I can cross the finish line and be both happy with my performance and thrilled to hear that my friend met her goal as well. I can high-five a total stranger or my training partner because both of us did what we set out to do. There need not be a muted celebration, a sheepish shrug at the net of a tennis match out of sensitivity to the competitor whose dreams have just been dashed. Your success is enhanced, not diminished, by the success of others. We can all rejoice together because my result does not come at the expense of yours.

Running, of course, is not just about the race-day experience. The journey of training for an event, or even running without ever racing, has countless rewards. You can feel healthier, both mentally and physically. You can outrun the demons, or the chocolate chip cookies, that are chasing you. You can get fitter or faster. You can lose weight. And you can draw on the support of others, and offer yours to them, as you both pursue your goals and dreams.

But it's remarkable to note that at the start line of a major race like Boston are tens of thousands of amateur runners, all of whom have not just a shot at glory but the opportunity to achieve it together. It's not that everyone has a chance to be the one person who is happy with the outcome. It's that there's a chance every single one of us will be happy at the same time.

As Bart Yasso says, all of us travel the same path to the finish line, but each of us takes a different one to the start. When the gun goes off, the route to Boylston Street is finite, clear and uninterrupted; there is only a handful of significant turns, and the entire course is carefully marked. The many trails to Hopkinton, however, can be twisting, meandering, intermittent, limitless and uncertain. For most runners, it's harder to get to the start of this marathon than to the finish.

That's part of the communal joy of gathering in the opening

corrals of a race like Boston. We all have our reasons for being here; each back story is remarkable and infinite. The day belongs to all of you, success is in abundance, and nothing you gain comes at a cost to anyone else. The final journey is not made alone. And you are surrounded not by rivals but by kindred spirits.

# CHAPTER 43

On an April morning in Boston, almost any weather is possible. On this particular morning, it's cold and windy and the forecast is calling for rain. It's one of the coolest Patriots' Days in the past decade.

It could be worse: it isn't scorching hot and the air isn't heavy with humidity, as it has been many times in Boston Marathon history. Of course, there have been many editions with moderate and even ideal running conditions, when the race has been more memorable than the weather. The odds of a mild day with overcast or partly cloudy skies are pretty high in the early spring in Boston. But in more than a century of racing, the unusual events accumulate and are more likely to stick in the memory than unremarkable conditions. So Boston has developed a reputation for unusual weather.

It's partly deserved. From one year to the next, the conditions at the Boston Marathon can range from unbearably humid to brutally cold. Over the course of one hundred and twenty years, runners have been greeted by temperatures from below freezing to the high nineties. There have been snow squalls and gusting winds traveling faster than the elite athletes. There has been mist and sleet and torrential rain. There have been threatening skies and even a partial eclipse of the sun.

Also, while the average temperature on race day in Boston is in the low fifties, similar to big races in Chicago, New York and Washington, Boston experiences more extremes. According to analysis done by *Runner's World* magazine, the spread between the average lowest and average highest race-day temperatures between 2000 and 2012 was twenty-five degrees. None of the others had a span greater than eighteen. So the conditions are more likely to change during the course of the race in Boston.

And then there's the wind. Running from west to east, toward the ocean, you are more likely to have it in your face than at your back. One exception was in 2011, when Geoffrey Mutai ran the fastest marathon in history, taking advantage of a Hopkinton-to-Boston tailwind of fifteen to twenty miles per hour to finish in 2:03:02.

On about half-a-dozen occasions, there has been sleet or snow. The Boston Marathon website lists three instances of driving rain. In 2002 a heavy mist reduced visibility and kept helicopters on the ground, which hampered the television coverage of the race.

And then there's the heat. High temperatures were a particular factor before the start was moved to the morning. Until 2007, race time was at noon, meaning the runners would often be traveling the course in the warmest part of the day. In 1905, there were reports the temperature exceeded 100. Four years later, it hit 97.

At the 1927 marathon, the temperature was in the mid-80s. The previous year, Johnny Miles, a 20-year-old delivery boy from Canada who was wearing tennis shoes, had upset both Clarence DeMar and the reigning Olympic champion, Albin Stenroos of Finland, in a course-record time. A banner headline on the front page of the Boston Post proclaimed: "Unknown Kid Smashes Record in Greatest of All Marathons." Miles was honored at a series of speaking engagements and personal appearances.

But the next year he would be the subject of scorn and ridicule for wilting in the heat. In fact, what really happened was that his father had devised new shoes for the race. According to a book about Canadian participants in Boston by David Blaikie, the elder Miles trimmed the soles of his son's shoes to make them lighter. The pair figured it would make a repeat title almost a certainty. "Nothing to it, just a walk-away," Miles said.

Miles never wore the shoes until the day of the Boston Marathon. With the sun beating down on the road, Miles immediately began to feel the heat in his soles. The newly finished road out of Hopkinton was, according to Blaikie, beginning to bubble.

"Before I got three miles the blood was coming through my sneakers, these little canvas shoes," Miles said. "I lost the toenails on both feet, big blisters coming up under each one of them. I tried to pull my toes up because the sock was pulling on the nails. Then the top of the toes skinned off and blistered. My feet were just a mass of blood."

He dropped out at seven miles, and DeMar went on to claim his fifth title. Photos show DeMar soaked in sweat at the finish, a kerchief tied neatly to his head. The same newspapers that had vaunted Miles a year earlier now brutalized him, portraying him as a quitter and a bad champion. Fortunately, Miles found redemption two years later when he returned to Boston and won a second time.

The mercury has hit the eighties or nineties about once a decade throughout Boston Marathon history. In 1976, America's bicentennial year, the temperature along some parts of the course rose into the high nineties. More than forty percent of participants dropped out before the finish. The race became known as the "run for the hoses."

In 2012, with the forecast calling for temperatures in the mid-eighties, organizers issued thorough warnings days before the race and offered runners the option of deferring their participation to the following year. By midday, the temperature had climbed to eighty. The average finishing time dropped by almost half an hour.

There will be nothing like that to contend with this year. The temperature as we board the bus in Boston is in the low forties. For the race, I'm wearing shorts and two layers of t-shirt, a short-sleeve on top of a long-sleeve. I have a winter hat and a pair of gloves. On top of my running gear I'm sporting a hoodie and a pair of sweatpants that I can throw away at the start. My wife picked them up at a discount clothing store for a total of seven dollars.

Fortunately, Bob has brought along a couple of rain ponchos that we can slip into to help stay dry. The greatest challenge today might be staying warm and dry before the race begins.

# CHAPTER 44

For 364 days of the year, Hopkinton has a population of about 15,000. It's like many other New England towns: quaint and quiet, with a few thousand homes, a red-brick town hall, and an annual town meeting at which residents vote directly on the budget and other important issues.

But for one morning each April, the 300-year-old village is invaded by the strangest-looking army in the world, tens of thousands of numbered individuals wearing shorts and t-shirts underneath garbage bags, blankets, pyjama pants and sweatshirts. One bus after another arrives and unloads its human cargo. Although they are friendly and well-intentioned, these 30,000 visitors are the worst possible guests. They eat, drink, and go to the bathroom multiple times, wherever they can find a convenient spot indoors or outdoors. And it's clear they can't wait to leave; they check their watches regularly and talk excitedly about how they will spend the rest of the day somewhere else. Within a few hours, they are all gone, having run out of the town as quickly as possible. After a day of cleanup, everything in Hopkinton returns to normal.

The organizers of the 1908 Olympic marathon in London had no idea what they were doing to and for the people of Hopkinton, Massachusetts when they changed the length of the marathon course to twenty-six miles, three hundred and eighty-five yards. Hopkinton just happens to be twenty-six miles west of Boston, so when the Boston Athletic Association decided in 1924 to have its annual marathon conform to what had become the standard distance, the starting line was moved to Hopkinton.

"Hopkinton is the epitome of small-town America," four-time winner Bill Rodgers says in a Boston Marathon video. "It's the perfect place, I think, to start the world's greatest marathon." The town website proclaims, appropriately, "It all starts here."

You are dropped at the athletes' village, on the grounds behind the local middle school and high school. On a normal day, this is home to a few hundred students from the surrounding twenty miles. But on this holiday Monday, some 30,000 people from more than eighty countries have gathered here.

There are volunteers everywhere, wishing you luck. Some of them applaud as you walk through the village. If you're fortunate, you squeeze into an empty spot under one of the three large white tents that are set up on the school grounds. If you remember to bring something to sit on, like a garbage bag or a towel, you spread it out. You try to find a comfortable position to sit in, given that it's the cold ground of April and you are about to run for hours.

On this particular Marathon Monday, you are bundled up, but you are ready for anything. There are volunteers handing out orange-and-pink fleece hats from Dunkin Donuts. You look around and see people huddled in pajamas and onesies, hats and scarves, all waiting for the appointed hour. You remind yourself that in other years the runners have been through worse.

It's too early for a lot of chatter, but you do meet other runners and exchange a few stories. It's a collegial atmosphere combined with lots of nervous energy. In the background, regular announcements are repeated regularly over a loudspeaker. More buses are emptying out.

And then, finally, your wave is called. You leave the school grounds, passing under a banner that wishes you luck, and you march north on Grove Street. The streets are fenced off, separating runners from spectators and residents. It's not clear how the residents of Hopkinton get to where they are going on Marathon Monday, unless they just wait until all of us are gone.

You walk about half a mile up the road. To your left, the parking lot behind the pharmacy is ringed by more than a hundred portable toilets. It's the last-chance rest stop before the start line.

You make a right onto Main Street. This is the last turn you will make until after the halfway point in the race. You are now on Route 135, the road that will take you through Ashland, Framingham, and Natick. You find the corral that corresponds to your qualifying time.

Your visit to Hopkinton is almost over. You're now approaching the northeastern corner of town. There are announcements and a countdown. After the long, slow hours of waiting in the athletes' village, the minutes are suddenly flying by.

It continues to be cold and rainy, but you don't care. The extra clothes are helping, and in marathons, too cold is always better than too hot. Once you are moving, the rain won't matter.

The gun goes off and the thousands of runners in front of you begin to move up toward the start line. You shuffle past the salon, the antique store and the town hall. You pass in front of Bill's Pizza and Restaurant, the bank, the Masonic lodge, the Korean Presbyterian church. You file past a small cemetery. On your right is a cute little three-acre downtown park. A short road breaks off Main Street to the east. It's called Marathon Way, even though it's not actually part of the course and is only two hundred feet long, less than the shortest sprint distance in the Olympics.

And then, just before the corner of Ash Street, with a stately white building on your right where the Boston Marathon offices are located, you cross over a work of art, the painted blue-and-yellow line created each year for more than three decades by Jacques LeDuc. You are stepping into more than a hundred years of history, into a race that may be run for hundreds of years to come. You're joining more than 575,000 runners who have traveled this path before.

With some ten thousand miles behind you, you have just over twenty-six to go. You are now running the Boston Marathon.

# CHAPTER 45

After the long bus ride, the hours of waiting, the slow march through Hopkinton, it is a simple pleasure to be moving. I came here, after all, not to sightsee, not to meet people, not to wander, but to run. In a few hours, it will take all of my willpower to continue to put one foot in front of the other. But now I am sailing downhill, enjoying the electric atmosphere, the freedom of movement, the tree-lined rural New England streets.

Just before the race started, it began to rain. But once I started moving, that wasn't of much concern. I quickly discarded my plastic rain poncho and some of my extra clothes. I am now wearing just the long-sleeve shirt under my t-shirt, a winter hat, shorts and a pair of gloves.

A joyful roar went up as the race began. Like many runners in front of and behind me, I hit a button on my watch as I crossed the start line and then threw my hands in the air. For a race with 30,000 runners and more than a century of history, the start area is surprisingly modest. There is no archway, just small section of bleacher seats for spectators and a few vertical banners of yellow and blue on either side of the painted line that marks the beginning of the race.

The first few hundred yards of road are narrow for a big-city race, one of the main reasons why Boston has to restrict its field of participants. At the start line, the route is less than forty feet across. More than running a race, you are being herded along at the pace of everyone around you, like fans exiting a ballpark and shuffling toward a subway station. But it feels good to be part of a throng of humanity celebrating movement and endurance. And the volume of runners mitigates the urge to sprint downhill in the early yards of the race.

Near the end of the second mile, you pass a small sign on the side of the road, in front of a white fence. *Entering Ashland*. This is the site of the starting line for the first twenty-seven editions of the Boston Marathon. If the British royal family had never demanded a different course in London in 1908, causing the marathon distance to be extended, the race might only now be starting, just a few blocks away from the current course. You don't feel the extra distance now, when your legs and the euphoria of the start are still fresh. It's at the other end of the race when you curse King Edward and Queen Alexandra.

Instead of having the attention Hopkinton receives every April, Ashland simply lays claim to its place in history with a few plaques at Marathon Park on Pleasant Street, where Metcalf's Mill once stood. One of the signs bears the slogan "It all started here," a clear contrast in tense to the motto employed by the Town of Hopkinton, "It all starts here." Marathon Park also refers to itself as "cradle of the worldwide running boom." Ashland is home to an annual half-marathon held about a month before Patriots' Day and described by organizers as the "perfect prep" for the Boston Marathon. But marathon runners only pass through Ashland today; they don't start here.

As the course opens up, the varying paces of the runners become more evident. The mass of bobbing heads breaks into smaller pieces. There are runners zooming past you and others to whom you catch up quickly. There are groups traveling together. You start to see the colorful shirts, the costumes, the nametags, the t-shirts from fundraising causes and other races.

In other large marathons, you run all over a big city. In the early minutes of this one, it feels like you are running through America. In Ashland and Framingham and Natick, you pass houses, farms, churches and temples, small businesses, restaurants, gas stations, community centers, dollar stores, hair salons, ATMs, billboards. You see manicured lawns and wild grass and white picket fences and mailboxes and flags and bunting. You are running through everyday life. You move by TJ's Food and Spirits, the Mobil station, the Dunkin

Donuts, the Tasty Treat, the Honey Dew, the CVS pharmacy, the Shell, the clock tower, the Cherry Blossom Chinese Cuisine, the pizza palace, the car wash. In Framingham, you cross the train tracks where, a century before, the race leaders were forced to stop.

In every parking lot, there is a crowd gathered, a band playing or speakers blaring recorded music. The sounds of the runners – the breaths, the footfalls, the quick gasps of conversation – give way to the volume of the supporters. In the rain, they are gathered still. They stand on hills, on sidewalks, on balconies, on flatbed trucks. They lean out windows. They clap, they shout, they hold up signs. But mostly they watch the river of runners flow through their small towns. The difference between a race and a run is not the clock, but the crowd. You are racing against time, but with the people.

# CHAPTER 46

There are many aspects of completing a marathon that are simple, wholesome and pure. Passing through the Wellesley Scream Tunnel is not one of them. This is the noisiest, friendliest and raunchiest part of the Boston course.

Wellesley is a small liberal arts college for women that was founded in 1870 and accepted its first students five years later, more than two decades before the first Boston Marathon. It just happens to be located at about the halfway point of the marathon, making it an appropriate spot for a loud and boisterous cheering section and, as is now the custom, a few dozen offers of gratuitous affection.

According to college lore, some Wellesley students shouted encouragement to the Harvard frontrunner Dick Grant in the very first Boston Marathon. Indeed, the *Boston Globe* account from 1897 says "several young women from Wellesley" received the leaders, "and when they recognized the Harvard colors of Grant they cheered." I doubt they were holding provocative signs or demanding kisses, but on that day a tradition appears to have been born, one that has evolved into the most famous segments of any marathon course in the world.

College students have been turning out on Marathon Monday for more than a century. The number of spectators began to flourish exponentially in the 1970s, when women were officially allowed to enter the race. And in keeping with the times, their behavior began to change as well.

This is not a place for polite applause or chaste words of encouragement. You can hear the screams from hundreds of yards away, building to a deafening crescendo by the time you arrive at the campus. At that point, the race suddenly takes on a different patina. Instead of drawing on the energy of the crowd to power through the halfway point or simply waving at the spectators, many runners slow down to read the hundreds of hand-painted signs, high-five some students and kiss others. The field tends to drift to the right, where the women of Wellesley hang over the barricades and offer their hands, cheeks and lips. It's like a marathon being run through freshman orientation week.

According to Mark Sullivan, a Pennsylvanian who has completed Boston thirty years in a row, the women used to line both sides of the road, but that really created a tunnel effect as they encroached on the course to touch the runners.

There are too many signs, affixed to the metal barricades or held by the boisterous students, to read on the run. But even at a quick glance, the recurring theme becomes obvious. "What's the rush? Kiss me." "Kiss me, I'm Italian." "Kiss me, I'm from California." "Kiss me, I'm a mathematician." "Kiss me – I won't tell your wife." "Your pace or mine?" "Kiss me – I'll make you run faster." "Stamina turns me on." There are a few signs that cross into even more risqué territory than that.

But there are other banners as well, many of which are more about the marathon. The students accept orders in advance of the race so that if you know someone who is running, you can request some encouraging words to spur them on. The names of hundreds of runners are painted on cardboard by young women who have never even met them. The Wellesley Scream Tunnel has its own Facebook page and Twitter account.

It's hard to believe the total student population is less than 2,500; it feels like three times that many spectators crowd into that quarter of a mile. In those two minutes, I receive more offers of affection than I did in my entire adolescence and young adulthood. I respectfully decline all of them and stick to high-fives, virtuously carrying on to the halfway point in the race.

## CHAPTER 47

So what's the big deal about Heartbreak Hill? It's the most famous peak on a marathon course in the world – in fact, it's probably the only hill on any marathon course that you've ever heard of. But it's actually not that steep, nor is it particularly distinct on the Boston Marathon course. Many runners ascend it and then a few minutes later ask a runner next to them, "How long until we get to Heartbreak Hill?"

This part of the course is certainly not easy, but the hill itself doesn't stand out on its own unless you are looking for it. Heartbreak Hill is the last of the four Newton Hills, which begin about sixteen miles into the race. Because the race has been mostly downhill until that point, and because it's the second half of the marathon and runners are starting to get tired, Newton is considered one of the toughest sections of the Boston Marathon.

Before you even get to Heartbreak Hill, you must pass through another ominously named portion of the course: Hell's Alley. As you leave Wellesley, you cross over Route 128, also known as the Yankee Division Highway. Route 128 is a partial beltway around Boston that includes Interstate 95. You could make a wrong turn here and, assuming you had enough energy gels, run all the way to Florida.

Just before the overpass, the course climbs about fifty-five feet in about one mile. A volunteer described to the *Boston Globe* what she has witnessed from her vantage point at a first-aid station at the top of the hill. "I've seen hyperthermia, hypothermia, hyponatremia, heart attack, diabetic emergencies, falls, sprains, blisters, diarrhea, vomiting," she said. "I've seen it all on this hill."

"Everybody talks about the hills, but this is where the real race starts," Bill Rodgers, the four-time Boston champion, told the *Globe*.

At the bottom of the hill, you pass the Newton-Wellesley Hospital, where a few race dropouts have been taken after succumbing to

Hell's Alley. And then you make the famous right turn at the Newton Fire Station and begin to climb the Newton Hills.

Heartbreak Hill comes at precisely the point when many runners are hitting the wall. The marathon has often been described as twenty miles of hope and six miles of truth. Heartbreak Hill arrives just after the twenty-mile marker. Over the space of less than half a mile, the course rises by just under ninety feet. That's a bit of a climb but it shouldn't be enough to break your heart or crush your legs. One estimate put the grade at just over three percent. There are lots of races that have much steeper ascents and they don't have depressing names attached to them.

That's because the name arises not from the hill but the despair that happened on it. In 1936, Johnny Kelley was the popular defending Boston Marathon champion. On the second-last of the Newton Hills, he caught up to the lead runner, a Native American named Ellison Brown, who was known as both Tarzan and Deerfoot. The year before, Brown had finished in thirteenth place, even though his shoes fell apart on the course and he had to run the final five miles barefoot.

In 1936, Brown ran a blistering pace, so much so that apparently the driver of the press vehicle didn't even realize he was in the lead and was following Kelley instead. But Kelley managed to catch up to Brown, and as he passed the frontrunner, he gave him a reassuring pat on the shoulder, by way of apology or consolation for overtaking him. As the story goes, the gesture sparked something in Brown, who rallied and regained the lead from Kelley. According to some reports from the time, the two swapped places several times in the next few hundred yards, with Kelley overtaking Brown on the uphills and Brown surging ahead on the downhills. Brown finally prevailed and Kelley fell to fifth place.

Sports columnist Jerry Nason covered the race for the *Boston Globe* and wrote about how Brown broke Kelley's heart on the final hill in Newton. For eighty years, the name has persisted.

Sixty-six years later, at the age of ninety-four, Kelley told the *Boston Globe* he lamented tapping Brown on the shoulder. "I made a big mistake when I did that," he said. "It was as much to say, hey, boy, move over. It was a terrible thing to do, and I still regret it."

Both Brown and Kelley represented the United States at the 1936 Olympics in Berlin. Brown, who was from the Narragansett tribe in Rhode Island, won a second Boston Marathon in 1939. He and Tom Longboat, the legendary Canadian runner, are the only two Native Americans to have won the race.

This residential section of the course is quite picturesque. Commonwealth Avenue is divided by a grassy island populated by trees. There are quaint homes and shops on both sides of the road. If you were to travel it by car or in Google Street View, you wouldn't notice much of an incline. But if you have to climb it twenty miles into a footrace, it's a little more evident.

Even so, Heartbreak Hill sounds more daunting than it really is. It's an important milestone on the course, and it's a place that draws strong and supportive crowds. If you need extra energy to conquer the Newton Hills, you can count on supporters to push you through. And the best thing about Heartbreak Hill is that once you've conquered it, it's mostly downhill and flat the rest of the way to the finish line.

# CHAPTER 48

Just when you think it's almost over, however, it's becomes very clear that it is not. You have summited Heartbreak Hill, yes. But you are still five miles from the finish. And you are now on the section of the course known as the Haunted Mile.

From Boston College to Cleveland Circle, you run past a cemetery which was labelled "the graveyard of champions" by Jerry Nason, the same Boston sportswriter who named Heartbreak Hill. Bill Squires, who coached Bill Rodgers, told the *Boston Globe* he referred to it as "the Cemetery of Lost Hope" because "so many bloody guys got there and were done."

Yes, this the part of the marathon course where all that hope and optimism you felt at the start are a distant memory. When you passed a cemetery before the start line it almost escaped your attention. Now it's a metaphor for the race and proof of the futility of life itself. And it also comes with a slight uphill, after you were promised that Heartbreak was the last climb of the race.

The Haunted Mile is where a reassessment takes place for many runners. You have finished the hardest part of the course. You have completed the twenty miles of hope. How do you feel as you start the six miles of truth? "You're either in a good spot at that time -- or you're in the graveyard," two-time winner Joan Benoit-Samuelson once said. "People either lose the race there or they start to regroup and rally and chase to the finish."

John Kelley didn't lose races just on Heartbreak Hill. Apparently he also fell behind half a dozen times in the Haunted Mile. And the second John Kelley, who won the race in 1957 but was no relation to the first, says there was a perception among runners that it was jinxed. "You would hear old-timers talk about how many people were leading at that point and folded up," said the younger Kelley.

"If there's a wall to be hit, you're going to hit it pretty soon."

In 1903, Sammy Mellor was said to be leading the race by almost a mile at the top of Heartbreak Hill. Then he started walking. According to the *Globe*, "His friends frantically implored the little New Yorker to begin again, but Mellor plaintively remarked that he could hardly move. The great crowd at Lake Street urged him on, and he gamely responded, but his collapse was but a question of time." A runner named John Lorden eventually caught up to and then passed Mellor. There are at least ten other cases in which the lead was reported to have changed hands in the Haunted Mile.

For ordinary runners, there's some logic to the idea that the mile after Heartbreak is a tough one. If you pushed too hard trying to prove yourself on the legendary climb, you might have to pay back that debt on the other side (of the hill, not in the afterlife evoked by the cemetery).

There is something uniquely Bostonian about the fatalistic outlook toward and labelling of these crucial parts of the course. After all, for every lead surrendered on Heartbreak Hill, for every advantage lost in the Haunted Mile, there is a race won by another runner. In the zero-sum game of elite athletics, every defeat is the flip side of a victory. One runner's heartbreak is someone else's dream come true. What is haunted for some is hallowed ground for others.

Why isn't Heartbreak Hill named Rejuvenation Hill, from the perspective of Ellison Brown? Why isn't the Haunted Mile the Blessed Mile, invoking the angels from the cemetery who inspired the accelerating runners instead of the spooky ghosts who doomed the struggling? The younger John Kelley actually charged ahead of two legendary Ethiopian runners, Abebe Bikila and Mamo Wolde, to finish second in 1963.

Maybe it's a spillover from the Curse of the Bambino, which kept the Red Sox from winning the World Series for eighty-four years. Maybe it's because a marathon is such an inherently tough battle that it's easier to relate to it from the perspective of the person squandering the lead than gaining it. Even those who take the lead in the Haunted Mile know there is someone chasing them, and it could just as easily be they who are first depleted and then overtaken. From here to the finish, we are all just one step away from walking.

# CHAPTER 49

As a baseball fan since childhood, I can't remember the first time I saw the Citgo sign. Rising beyond the Green Monster at Fenway Park, it's an iconic image on the Boston skyline.

If it weren't such a part of the city's heritage, it might be criticized for being bland, commercial, and unattractive. It's a white background with a simple, raised reddish-orange triangle (the company calls it a trimark) and the word Citgo printed below that in uppercase letters in a very plain font.

But over time, even an eyesore can become a heritage symbol. The sign has stood over Kenmore Square since 1965. So for more than fifty years, it has welcomed runners to the final stretch of the Boston Marathon course. Once you see the Citgo sign, you know you are approaching downtown Boston. The problem for runners is that the sign is so visible, it's almost an optical illusion. Once you spy it, it takes a long time to reach and pass it. The finish line is not as close as you would think.

Although it's now a major Boston symbol, the Citgo sign was almost taken down barely fifteen years after it was erected. During the oil crisis in 1979, the neon was turned off as a symbol of energy conservation. After it stood dark for four years, Robert Campbell of the *Boston Globe* argued the lights should be turned back on, calling the sign an "accidental masterpiece" in an article headlined "The Return of a Crown Jewel." Campbell said without the neon lights, the sign was "a scarecrow, a dead thing, a skull stuck on a stick."

"The Citgo sign," Campbell wrote, "is a landmark of Boston and of its time as legitimate as the State House dome. It stands for an important period in our history, the age of ebullience and optimism that followed World War II. It flags a major intersection in our city. And it's beautiful. Turning it off is the kind of easy gesture that does little to deal with the energy crisis but diminishes our lives. If signs are going to be turned off, Citgo should be the last in Massachusetts, not the first, to go."

But the sign was deteriorating and the company actually wanted to take it down. Like Campbell, many Bostonians would hear nothing of it. They protested and the billboard was restored, then refurbished again two decades later, the neon replaced with LED lights.

According to the Citgo website, there's a well-known expression in Boston: "London has Big Ben, Paris has the Eiffel Tower. Boston has the Citgo sign." I've never heard anyone in Boston actually say that, but the Lonely Planet website repeats this quotation, so it's not just marketing hyperbole. Having said that, the Citgo website doesn't hold back on its praise for the iconic image. "It's no secret that the Citgo sign in Boston's Kenmore Square is beloved by people across the country and around the world." You can even download Citgo sign wallpaper for your computer.

The sign is distinctively Boston, so much so that it's almost surprising to learn that Citgo is an oil business based in Houston and indirectly owned by the Venezuelan government. It's become so important to Boston that the sign has survived its original purpose. It no longer stands above a Citgo location; it's now purely a landmark.

The Citgo symbol is not the only sign on the Boston Marathon course that inspires you to keep going. All along the route, not just in Wellesley, spectators take the trouble to put their words of encouragement on paper and cardboard.

I'm not the sort of person who makes signs. I've stood at the finish line and along the course of many races, and I've certainly cheered and shouted encouragement. And I've been to hundreds of baseball, hockey and football games at which I've rooted for one team or another. But I've never been moved to pull out my markers and get crafty about the whole thing.

Thankfully, marathon spectators are much less inhibited than I about committing their words of encouragement to paper and cardboard rather than just shouting them at passing runners. Many signs along the course are supportive and inspiring. Some of them are hilarious. Others are just plain fun.

*Go, random stranger!*

*Thank you for running!*

*You're an inspiration!*

*You were made for greatness.*

*You run better than the government.*

*Hey you, nice legs!*

*Only 20 miles left.*

*Only 316,800 inches to go.*

*You run marathons. I watch them on Netflix.*

*Beer and bragging rights just ahead.*

*Toenails are for sissies.*

*Insert motivational phrase here.*

*Worst parade ever.*

*I won't lie. You aren't almost there.*

*Pain now, beer later.*

*It's not sweat. It's liquid awesome.*

*Pain is temporary. Internet race results last forever.*

*Suck it up, cupcake.*

*Run like someone called you a jogger.*

*It could be worse. You could be married to a Kardashian.*

*Baby you were born to run.*

*Chuck Norris never ran a marathon.*

When you finally get past the Citgo sign, the crowds get thicker and louder. The city begins to build up around you. You're back on Commonwealth Avenue. Just two more turns to go. The finish line is not far away now.

# CHAPTER 50

Poor Hereford Street. The 26.2 miles of the Boston Marathon course are dominated by Route 135, by Commonwealth Avenue, by Beacon Street. They are the workhorses of the course, the roads the runners respect, esteem, and even curse.

And then Boylston Street steps in at the end and gets all the glory. In between, Hereford just puts in a cameo appearance. It's so short it can't even lay claim to being the 385 yards, the 0.2 miles of this race. It's barely 600 feet before you are turning again, onto the scene-stealing Boylston. Hereford is the on-deck circle, the warm-up act, the undercard. It's not there. It's almost there.

Just before you get to the Hereford anteroom, a portion of Commonwealth Avenue dips under Massachusetts Avenue at the Tommy Leonard Bridge. The route beneath the underpass is one that many runners will recognize from the television coverage of the event. But they may not know much more about it than that.

The bridge is named after an octogenarian Bostonian and former marathon runner who once presided over the legendary Eliot Lounge, which stood for almost exactly half a century at the same corner. The Eliot opened in 1946 and soon became a popular post-war gathering place with cheap cocktails.

A former Marine, Tommy Leonard took over as the daytime bartender in 1972 and helped to turn the Eliot into a legendary sports bar. There are stories of golf champion Fuzzy Zoeller taking over behind the bar late into one night. Characters like Bill Lee of the Boston Red Sox were regulars. According to the *Boston Globe*, Lee would sometimes sneak into the bar during a rain delay at Fenway Park. Marching bands from visiting schools gave impromptu concerts in the bar.

A 2005 tribute to the Eliot in *Sports Illustrated* begins, "Once, there was a place where nobody batted an eye the night the horse walked in. The horse stopped to visit with everyone sitting at the bar, and then it took eight people to get him out again, and nobody in the place thought it at all remarkable, though they thought the horse well-behaved." Apparently the equine visitor was there to mark Tommy Leonard's fiftieth birthday.

Leonard was a runner and a big supporter of the Boston Marathon. He completed more than twenty marathons and founded the successful Falmouth Road Race. A photo of him finishing Boston appeared in *Sports Illustrated* in 1956. Because of his passion for running, the Eliot soon became the place to be on Marathon Monday. After passing the bar in the final few miles of the course, runners would return with the promise of a free beer from Leonard if they simply showed their bib numbers from the race. If the bar in the clubhouse at a golf course is the nineteenth hole, then the Eliot was the twenty-seventh mile of the marathon.

"I saw a gap," Leonard told the *Boston Globe* before the 2016 marathon. "I saw an opening, where runners should be able to get together and socialize. There was a need for that. When I used to run in the fifties, you got an apple, maybe, or a cup if you won, and then you were on your own. I wanted to bring people together."

For many years, the Eliot offered a one-dollar spaghetti dinner the night before the race and displayed the flags of all the countries represented in the marathon. Leonard put a countdown clock in the bar before the race and a walk of fame on the sidewalk in front of the lounge. In 1980, when Rosie Ruiz was discovered to have cheated to cross the finish line first, Leonard invited the true champion, Canadian Jacqueline Gareau, and her husband to the Eliot, where the patrons sang her national anthem and gave her roses.

The Eliot closed in 1996, but by then a fitting tribute had already been established. The bridge was rededicated to Leonard before the 2016 marathon.

"What I really wanted to do with the Eliot was extend some Beantown hospitality," Leonard said. "And I loved every second of it for twenty-five years. I met people from all over the world." Those people no longer gather at the Eliot, but they still pass under the Tommy Leonard Bridge, on their way to the final two turns of the Boston Marathon.

# CHAPTER 51

This is not reverie. This is Boylston Street, the most cherished half-mile in marathon running. It is the summit of Everest. It is Santiago's marlin. It is Homer's Ithaca (not the Homer who crosses Springfield Gorge).

The official start line is only twenty-five miles behind me, my home barely a ninety-minute flight from here. Yet I have traveled thousands of miles on foot, a passage that started years ago. Much of that journey was running in circles, until I finally sorted out the best way to get here.

I have been blessed with so much good fortune in my life, an embarrassment of riches, that dreams feel greedy. I dare not ask for more. On birthdays, I am the guy who is impossible to buy for: I have everything and want nothing. But this I have allowed myself to covet. I have craved this tableau for a long time. Beyond the health and happiness of my children, nothing has inspired more hope, stimulated more hard work, caused more doubt and disappointment, evoked more fear, courage, anxiety, determination, fancy, desperation, anticipation.

Once there was the woman I thought would never be with me. Then I married her. After that there was Boston. Nothing else has captured my imagination quite like this.

It is not of great consequence, of course. I could have survived without ever completing the Boston Marathon. It's just a silly race with nothing at stake for me except a box being ticked.

And yet it matters to me, on a level that I'm almost embarrassed to acknowledge. When something is far beyond your reach, it can easily be written off as impossible. But once it is just outside your grasp, you must have it. That which is almost achievable is so much more tempting, so much easier to taste than pure fantasy. It is harder to accept losing the Super Bowl on a last-second field goal than to get blown out in the first half. Once I got close enough to it, Boston was a siren's call that I could never block out. I can, therefore I must.

This, then, is my Olympics. This is my presidential election night. This is my lifetime achievement award. I have just hit the game-winning home run in the bottom of the ninth inning, and I am rounding third and heading for home.

I am running with my hands in the air, my feet barely touching the ground. After traveling crowded, narrow streets for more than three-and-a-half hours, I have turned onto this wide avenue in downtown Boston, the Boulevard of Woken Dreams.

There are other runners, of course, but they are blending into the background. It feels like the course belongs to me alone. I am waving at spectators, total strangers all of them. They are pointing at me and smiling, yelling, cheering. I am pumping my arms like an NFL linebacker exhorting the crowd to get even louder.

For the first time in a marathon the sight of the finish line does not make me want to speed up, to get the whole thing over with, end the agony or shave as many seconds as possible from my recorded time. It has taken an eternity to get here, but I am in no hurry for it to be over. The one race that demands of you a fast previous time, the one that can punish you for wasting even a few precious seconds, is the very marathon that you want to go on forever.

I may never do this again. Even if I do, it will not be like this delicious first experience. The journey has been extraordinary, empowering and meaningful. But the destination is sublime.

In the final steps of a thousand training runs, I have gone to this place in my imagination. Now I am actually here. This is my victory lap. Today, at last, I am finishing the Boston Marathon.

PART 7

# I WENT UP THERE ONE TIME!

*"Running! If there's any activity happier, more exhilarating, more nourishing to the imagination, I can't think of what it might be. In running the mind flees with the body, the mysterious efflorescence of language seems to pulse in the brain, in rhythm with our feet and the swinging of our arms."*

JOYCE CAROL OATES

# CHAPTER 52

Orson Welles once said, "We're born alone, we live alone, we die alone." I would add to that: We run alone.

In running, just as in life, we frequently travel alongside others. As I've already pointed out, they share the journey with us, enhance many of our experiences and provide meaningful support and treasured company. There is tremendous comfort and strength in numbers; the landmark moments of our lives – both divine and devastating – are infinitely improved by the presence of the people we care about most.

But ultimately, they may simply distract us from Welles's essential truth, making us feel for a time that we belong to something greater and are not completely in isolation. "Only through our love and friendship can we create the illusion for the moment that we're not alone," Welles said. Surrounded by other runners, we might convince ourselves that we are sharing the load, but the deception can last only so long. Our brains may be diverted, but our bodies still measure every mile.

It may sound gloomy, even melodramatic. But acknowledging the solitude of life and running needn't be discouraging. The more prepared we are for the reality of the lonely trail, the better we can handle it. And while we may value collaboration, it is still validating and satisfying to accomplish something entirely on our own, whether that's learning a new skill, mastering a professional challenge, or heading out the door for a one-hour run. As my infant daughter used to say when I offered her help, "No, I do it."

I often train with others, particularly my friend Bob. But I also spend a lot of time running alone. In the past, I've occasionally listened to music or podcasts to help pass the time. But more recently, I've done all my runs without any soundtrack or other entertainment. I find being alone with my thoughts for an hour or two to be healthy, refreshing and stimulating. In my life, it's the closest thing to meditation or therapy. I've composed letters, columns, chapters in my head while running (struggling to remember all the key points so I could write them down as soon as I burst through the door of my home). I've thought through challenging problems. I've dreamed up new business ideas. But mostly I've simply shut down and enjoyed the movement of my body and the sounds of whatever is around me.

Like many people with busy lives full of meetings and demanding, interrupting young children, I have come to cherish the solitude and learn from it. In addition to being good for my mental health, running alone is, I find, important preparation for the loneliest moments of a marathon.

In a race, you are surrounded by runners and spectators, and you might even share the entire course with a friend, but the challenge is completely individual. I take great joy in the community of runners, but no matter who is beside you or behind you, both physically and spiritually, it is your body and no one else's – your energy, your legs, your breath, your determination – that will carry you to the finish line. There simply is no other equipment, nor is there, beyond moral support, any teamwork. That is both the greatest difficulty and the most rewarding aspect of running; you have nothing else to draw on but your own strength and pluck, no one else to blame when it all goes wrong. But guess who gets all the credit when you succeed?

At the start of a marathon it may feel like we're all in it together, but by the late stages there is no doubt: despite all that camaraderie before the gun went off, you are now among a series of individuals competing against themselves and the clock. Running with others can trick your mind, creating the deception that time and miles are passing by quickly, but it won't fool your body. No matter who is around you, no matter how much support you have, your legs and lungs still travel alone. Whether you are wearing a watch or not, they know exactly how long you have been moving, and how fast.

When you cross into that valley of despair some time after twenty miles, there can be no comfort found from either friends or strangers. You may be reminded by others to dig deep, but only you can actually summon the power to continue. Only your own efforts, your own words, either in private thoughts or even spoken aloud, matter at this point in the race.

It's been said many times that you learn a lot about yourself in those most challenging moments of a long run or a marathon. When your determination conquers your physical limitations, you discover a toughness you always hoped was there. One of life's greatest tests and indicators is how comfortable you are in your own skin, how much you respect the person you've become. It's easy to discover the answer when you are truly on your own, particularly when you are struggling through a grueling challenge. You can take that measurement in the late miles of a marathon.

You finish the race surrounded by other runners, with hundreds of spectators, maybe even loved ones, cheering you on. But they briefly fade into the background as you cross the line. At the end of a marathon, I'm happy to see other people. I'm grateful for the support and compliments of volunteers. I'm quick to congratulate other runners. But it's a private mixture of joy and relief that comes first, before the shared celebration.

At this point, I am usually a little bit of a mess. The hours of effort have stripped away my defenses, my inhibitions, my willpower. Everything is fresh and raw: relief and jubilation, pain and pleasure, delight and introspection. My thoughts wander to the many sources of inspiration that have led me down this crazy path, to my family members, living and dead, who I know would be proud. But first and foremost, I must feel satisfied with my own performance. The person I most want to prove something to is myself. A strong and gratifying result can cure a year's worth of self-doubt.

My composure is held together by the finest of threads. The smallest kind word or gesture – even someone offering me a water bottle, let alone a medal – can cause the weakest brick in my wall to rupture. If I speak out loud, it's in a broken voice. Sometimes I don't cry, but I come very close. Other times, I am sobbing.

Like many good cries, my tears reflect not one sentiment, but the gathering and dispersal of many. Certainly there is joy and satisfaction, but it's also a sudden release of a long accumulation of tension and pressure, a dumping ground for a thousand grievances and insecurities, frustrations and disappointments, grief and regret. At the end of a marathon, I feel shattered into a million pieces. I am broken and must be rebuilt. I wrap myself in a foil blanket, for both warmth and childlike security, and step slowly into the future, putting one step at a time between me and the rewarding, validating, life-changing ordeal behind me.

By the time I see my wife, I will have regained some self-control. I'll briefly lose it again in her arms, but not with the same immediacy or magnitude. In the first hundred yards after the finish line, I let everything flow out of me. I normally pride myself on putting reason before passion, evidence before sentiment. But right now, I surrender completely to my feelings. This is part of the experience that makes the marathon unique. This is what makes you want to start over some day and go through it all again. For a few hours it was just me and my body. Now I am alone with the purest and rawest of emotions.

# CHAPTER 53

It's one thing to be in motion in the cool wind and rain, throwing one foot in front of the other, generating a bit of heat, motivated by the quest to fulfill a dream, ticking a box high up the bucket list, savoring the joy of a once-unachievable goal finally realized. It's another to be stationary under a drenched poncho hour after hour, no medal or achievement as your reward, yet still smiling warmly, cheering loudly, greeting thousands of strangers like each is the first soul you've encountered on Christmas morning.

I arrived in Boston in awe of the marathon. I left in appreciation of the volunteers and spectators. I barely cracked the top 15,000, but from the moment I eagerly boarded a school bus on Boston Common until I flopped onto my hotel bed seven hours later, I was treated like a champion. And so were the other 26,609 runners before and after me.

As we walked through Hopkinton to the start line, I don't know how many times someone said, "Have a great run." Through Ashland and Framingham and Natick and Wellesley and Newton there were relentless cheers and signs both poignant and funny. And just past the finish line, there was a hero's welcome and an unforgettable moment: an emotional reunion with a woman I'd never met.

The 2015 Boston Marathon was my victory lap. For more than two years, getting to the start line was my sole training objective. Only after I earned a spot in the world's most coveted race did I even think about the finish line.

Even then I pictured only those final few hundred yards up to and including that blue painted line on Boylston Street. Who knew that one of the most memorable events of the entire experience would come on the other side of it?

A few months before the race, I interviewed Tim Scapillato, a runner who was preparing for his fifteenth trip to Boston. A couple of days later, his wife Marian sent me a note. Marian is also a runner, but she has never qualified for Boston. Rather than simply tag along with her husband every year, she volunteers at the race, handing out medals at the finish line.

"Would love to connect with you in hopes that you choose me to present you your finisher's medal," she wrote.

It was an offer I couldn't refuse. Marian sent me instructions, including a hand-drawn map of the finish area. "Stay to your right. Look for the red cap with the white maple leaf." A few days before the marathon, she sent me another note. "Just do what you know how to do," she wrote. "Your medal will be in my hand waiting for you!"

I savored every moment of Boston, especially those final thousand steps, my hands high in the air, on Boylston. In the finishing chute, I was greeted by a dozen other volunteers. "Congratulations!" "Way to go!" "You did it!" You never would have guessed they'd said it 10,000 times before.

I found Marian quickly; once I introduced myself, she threw her arms around me. It was at that moment that it hit me: after all that training, racing, failing, qualifying, running, *I'd finally finished the Boston Marathon.*

I always knew I would cherish my first Boston experience. But I never imagined how much I'd be won over by the volunteers and the people of Massachusetts. The race was amazing, but it was Marian and her colleagues who stole the show and made my day.

It's not unusual for me to be emotional at the finish line, but under these circumstances I was a complete wreck. The marathon breaks you and leaves you raw, ready to experience fully joy and relief and, in this case, the warmth and generosity of a new friend.

# CHAPTER 54

The evening following a marathon, you celebrate. You find a good restaurant and have a big meal. You walk around proudly, congratulating other runners you see in the street. You might even wear your medal as you travel about the town.

You watch the race highlights on the evening news. There are countless inspiring stories among the finishers. You watch a special display of sportsmanship and goodwill as defending men's champion Meb Keflezighi, on his way to eighth place this year, sprints to catch up to another elite athlete, Hilary Dionne, just so he could grab her hand and raise it as they crossed the finish line together.

And then you go back to the hotel and try to get some sleep. You savor the experience. You tell yourself you did it, you ran the Boston Marathon. But you don't think about the fact that there's a man who is still out there, trying to complete the race, making his way slowly toward the finish line you and almost 30,000 other athletes crossed many hours earlier.

The next morning, you learn about him on the local television news. His name is Maickel Melamed. He is thirty-nine years old, and he is from Venezuela. And he finally completed the marathon at about 4:00 a.m., almost twenty hours after he started.

Melamed has generalized muscle hypotonia, a condition similar to muscular dystrophy. He has very low muscle tone, a result of being born with the umbilical cord wrapped around his neck. As if that weren't enough misfortune on the first day of a new life, when doctors tried to give him oxygen, the tank was empty. He was not expected to live more than a few days.

Instead, he flourished, in his own remarkable way. He eventually became an academic, studying economics, philosophy and psychotherapy. He began paragliding, parachuting, diving, and mountain climbing. He ascended Venezuela's highest mountain, Pico Bolivar. And in 2009, he started running, at first traveling five hundred meters. He kept going until he could finish a seven-kilometer race, then a 10k, then a marathon. He ran Berlin, Chicago, New York and Tokyo, four of the six world majors. He was determined to run Boston, he said, because he had been sent there for treatment as a child.

All the runners contended with wind and rain at the 2015 Boston Marathon, but Melamed did it for fifteen or sixteen hours longer than most. And the weather only got worse as the day and night progressed. By the time he got to twenty-three miles, it was pouring. His muscles were aching. According to a report in the *Boston Globe*, at twenty-four miles, he began to doubt whether he would finish. "But the crowd that had stuck with him into the early morning saw him flag and began counting his steps aloud, the rhythm of their voices carrying him forward."

Not every story is as unlikely as Melamed's. But a marathon is a gathering of improbable heroes. In 2015, many of the participants raised money for the Martin Richard Foundation, a charity named after the eight-year-old victim of the bombings in 2013. A teacher from his school, a woman who had never run more than three miles before she started training for the marathon, was one of them.

Among the tens of thousands of runners were those who had overcome injury, loss of limb, illness, obesity, disease, tragedy, grief. There were others raising amounts of money great and small for hospitals, children's programs, women's shelters. There were people running for the people they'd lost, for their children, for their grandchildren, for hope, for the future. And then there were those for whom a marathon simply proved a point. *I can do it if I try.*

Legendary runner Joan Benoit-Samuelson, who won Boston twice, told a local television station that the most powerful journey in a marathon is not necessarily the fastest. "For me, the most inspiring stories come at the back of the pack," she said. "So if you're not up front with the elite athletes, don't worry about it. You have a story to tell, go out and tell it, and really just enjoy the journey and the experience."

We each have our own reason for running a marathon, for running hundreds of miles to prepare, for calling on every ounce of energy and every scrap of determination to complete our quest. It's almost impossible to finish a marathon without at least some preparation, so no one arrives at the starting line by accident. These are not whims or larks. The start line is not the beginning of the process. It's the beginning of the end.

"In any marathon, you have to know why you're doing it," Melamed said after he crossed the finish line. "Because in the last mile, the marathon will ask you."

We look at stories like Melamed's and we wonder if we could be the same unstoppable force. In some way, running is our statement that we would fight back just as hard as Melamed if we were confronted with the same headwinds, in life and on the marathon course. When you become a runner, when you complete a marathon, you define yourself as someone who won't stop until the job is done. If it takes longer than you expected, if it rains, if you cramp up, if your legs fail you, you'll keep going. The finish line must be crossed, one way or another, now or later.

Most of us are never tested quite like Maickel Melamed. But we are all smaller versions of him, pushing toward that finish line no matter what is pushing back against us.

# CHAPTER 55

On the day after the marathon, my wife Ginny and I played a little game while moving about Boston: How high could we count before we encountered someone wearing a Boston Marathon jacket?

Walking (hobbling, really) to the Museum of Fine Arts. One, two, three – here's a jacket.

Wandering (slowly) around the narrow streets of the North End. One, two, three, four – there's another one.

Sitting (that feels better) on a bench on Boston Common. One – oh, that guy over there is wearing one.

We never got past six.

It's a testament to two things. One, on Patriot's Day weekend, the running community basically takes over Boston. And two, the jacket has become the ultimate status symbol in marathon running.

Of course, we were traveling mostly in tourist areas less than 24 hours after the race. It might have been a different story in Cambridge or Brookline. But near the hotels and museums, runners were everywhere. And so was the jacket. Over the years, the Boston Marathon jacket has turned into a bit of a thing. It's become the ultimate souvenir from the most exclusive big-city marathon in the world. It's probably the most cherished item of clothing in the nation of runners. I don't know what the official numbers are, but it seems like somewhere in the neighborhood of three-quarters of Boston participants purchase one.

The race is over in a few hours, surviving only in memory. The t-shirt is nice, but it's probably best worn while running or lounging about on weekends. The medal is special, but it's going to spend a lot more time in a drawer or, if you get around to it, hanging on a wall rather than around your neck. It's not like you're going to wear it to work (okay, maybe once or twice).

The jacket, however, is a more useful memento. It's a windbreaker, so you can wear it in spring or fall, in all manner of circumstances. Going for a walk on a breezy evening? Throw on the Boston Marathon jacket. Cheering on runners at a fall race? I'll just grab my Boston jacket.

Like any souvenir clothing, putting it on allows you to relive the moment, to cherish your achievement. But let's be honest: it's a tiny bit pretentious and braggy. It's a status symbol among marathoners, a Rolex watch, a Chanel handbag. It's driving a BMW and wearing a leather BMW jacket, just in case people didn't see you actually getting out of your car.

We might as well be wearing a tag that says: "You know what I did last April?!" The Boston jacket is a statement or, more accurately, a billboard. *Oh, this old thing? Yes, as a matter of fact, I did run the Boston Marathon. Thanks for inquiring, after I made it pretty obvious that I wanted you to.*

If it were the jacket from any other race, it wouldn't feel as much like showing off. You don't have to qualify to run Philadelphia or San Diego. But Boston is an exclusive club. Wearing the jacket says you've joined the fraternity. It's like wearing a Mensa t-shirt. Or a Harvard law jacket. Is there a windbreaker for the billionaires on Forbes's list? Do ex-presidents have jackets with their dates in office embroidered on them?

On top of everything else, the jacket is, to put it mildly, hard to miss. It's typically bright and loud. The 2015 edition was purple with orange and white stripes. An earlier version was highlighter orange.

Even before we got to Boston, there were Boston jackets all around us. On the flight in, and in Logan Airport upon our arrival, we saw dozens of jackets from previous years. Traveling to the Boston Marathon while wearing a jacket from a previous year is a way of confirming the purpose of your trip to anyone else who's wondering about it. It's also a method of saying, "I've done this before!" I noticed some people had taken the trouble to embroider all the different years they'd run the race on the jacket, from their first appearance.

Look, there's nothing wrong with picking out a suitable keepsake from a milestone achievement. You earned it (and on top of that, you've paid for it). And I'll admit it: I gave into the temptation and bought one too. Mostly for research purposes, of course. You know, so I could write about it.

And yes, I wore it all over Boston on the Tuesday and Wednesday after the marathon. And okay, I threw it on as I went to work on my first day home. All right, I've also had it on dozens of times since then as well.

I do feel a bit self-conscious about it. Not quite enough to stop me from wearing it, though.

# CHAPTER 56

Thank you, Boston Athletic Association, for sending the email I coveted for more than two years, officially confirming my entry into the marathon.

Thanks, race officials, for expanding the field enough that I survived the cut-off. I can't imagine how heartbreaking it would be to run a qualifying time, but not get into the race.

Thank you Rick, my friend and coach, for believing in me and prescribing all of those fast, long runs that made me believe in myself.

Thank you, health gods, for allowing me to run (I'd give up a dozen Boston Marathons just to be allowed to run regularly for the rest of my life) and giving me the chance to run more than twenty marathons with only a few aches and pains. I'm blessed.

Thank you, Mom and Dad, for even though you weren't into sports or athletics yourself, you passed on genes that were good enough for me to run just as fast as I needed, and you taught me to chase my goals with ambition and persistence.

Thank you, all the runners and non-runners in my life, who indulged my dream, asked me about Boston, and wished me luck before I left for the race.

Thanks, other runners on the plane, who made me feel like I was in Boston the instant I boarded. We took up at least half the seats on the small flight, and I felt like the adventure had finally begun.

Thank you, hotel staff, for offering to move me to a higher floor, farther away from the noise of the theater district, so I could get a good night's sleep on the eve of the marathon.

Thank you, mayor of Boston, for the goodwill speech you delivered on behalf of the city at the pasta supper the night before the race. It was starting to lose its freshness by the fourth time they replayed it on the monitors, but I still appreciated the sentiment.

Thank you, volunteers shepherding us on the edge of Boston Common, for wishing us luck as we boarded the buses to the start line. Your energy at 7:30 in the morning was infectious.

Thank you, people of Hopkinton, for letting race officials take over your town with fencing and road closures and portable toilets and throwaway clothing. For one day a year, you welcome two guests for every person who lives in your town, and you treat them like royalty.

Thanks, unnamed members of the first corral, for offering us your tarp to sit on in the athletes' village when you departed for the start line.

Thank you, rain, for holding off until just before we started moving and for proving I'd put up with anything to achieve my goal.

Thank you, public works officials who painted the mile markers on the road the last time it was repaved. You know you're running a historic race when the milestones are permanent.

Thank you, two guys standing on the flatbed of a pickup truck outside the gas station in Framingham. There was something so honest, true, blue-collar, beer-commercial American about seeing you at the side of the route. You may not be running in this marathon, but I could tell you knew the value of hard work and commitment.

Thank you, spectators who stood in the pouring rain and still looked like you were having fun cheering us on.

Thanks, all you kids along the route who extended your hands for a quick tap as I passed by.

Thank you, aid station volunteers. How many times did you say "water" or "Gatorade" that one day? I don't think you get as much credit as you deserve, for yours is as great an endurance test as any marathon.

Thanks but no thanks, all you young women of Wellesley who offered, verbally or through signage, to inspire me to complete the second half of the course by doing mostly unspeakable and inappropriate things to me. Those were generous offers, and perhaps at another time I might have accepted. But the last time a complete stranger kissed me, I was a baby. So I'll stick to high-fives instead.

Thank you, cherished training partner, for sharing this remarkable journey for the past decade we've been running together, for showing me the way to Boston and for traveling the first fifteen miles of the race exactly as we've done during a thousand training runs, side-by-side, exchanging encouraging words and taking joy in each other's success.

Thank you, fellow runners, for sharing the road, cheering each other on, telling stories, greeting strangers, and delivering so much inspiration just by taking one step after another on this long adventure that began way before the start line. It was an honor to run with you. Respect.

Thank you, total stranger at about the twenty-first mile, for looking me directly in the eye, pointing at me with the ferocity of a university basketball coach, and exhorting me to go on.

Thank you and bless you, all those wearing Boston Strong t-shirts or holding signs that spoke of resilience. Your city knows more about toughness and durability than 10,000 visiting runners.

Thank you, Jack and Kate, for cheering me at the end of training runs and somehow understanding this was something I needed to do. I thought of both of you during the most challenging part of the race, hoping to make you proud by pushing hard all the way to the finish.

Thank you, forgiving runner, for being so understanding when I almost hit you in the face as I started pumping my arms to encourage the crowd with about two miles to go. You were pretty cool about that, considering I almost knocked the hat off your head.

Thank you, denizens of Boylston Street, for giving me one of the loudest receptions of my life. I honestly wouldn't have expected more if I were winning the Olympic Marathon in my hometown.

Thanks to one volunteer after another at the finish line, for congratulating me, offering me food and warmth and love and support like I was a lone lost traveller turning up on your doorstep.

There are a million companies in North America that provide much more indifferent service to fewer customers at a much higher cost. You made me cry.

Thank you, dear wife, partner, and best friend for looking so genuinely happy for me and throwing your arms around my sweaty body when we were reunited at the corner of Boylston and Arlington. You've indulged and supported this crazy obsession of mine for years, and it would mean so much less if you weren't there to share the journey with me.

Thanks again, hotel staff, for giving me a smoothie and a laurel wreath the second I walked through the door after the race. You've got right of first refusal on all my future visits to Boston.

Thank you, waiter in the fancy restaurant, for congratulating me on my run. I made it easy for you by showing off in my Boston Marathon jacket that evening, and I was hardly your only customer in that category, but you went out of your way to make me feel special.

Thank you, social media friends, for all the messages of encouragement before, during, and after the race. I'm grateful for your generosity of spirit, and I'd be lying if I pretended I didn't enjoy the attention.

Thanks, race organizers, for organizing a flawless and superb race for the runners. I don't know how you pull it off.

Thank you, Boston, for everything. I'd say you gave me a once-in-a-lifetime experience, but I'm not ruling out doing it all over again.

# CHAPTER 57

That's the inevitable question. Having finished the Boston Marathon and having shared my joy with anyone who would listen, I am asked regularly, "Are you going back?"

I'm tempted to use a variation on the answer that Jim Morrison once gave to a group of angry television producers. The Doors had just appeared on the legendary *Ed Sullivan Show* for the first time. They had been instructed to change the lyrics of their song "Light My Fire" from "Girl, we couldn't get much higher" to "Girl, we couldn't get much better" to avoid any implication that the line was about drugs.

Morrison went ahead and sang the original lyrics. After the show, the Doors were told by Sullivan's producers that they had planned to invite the band back for six more appearances, but because the group didn't cooperate, they would never do the Sullivan show again. Morrison apparently responded, "Hey man, we *just did* the Sullivan show."

*I just did the Boston Marathon*, I felt like saying. Do I need to do it again? The answer is that I don't know.

In the aftermath of Boston, I certainly continued running. But I made no immediate plans. For more than seven years, I had a dream. For more than two years I had only one goal. After Boston, it was time to exhale. In the weeks that followed, I settled into a nice rhythm, running five or six times a week and simply enjoying the pleasure of moving and staying in shape.

Of this I'm sure: there are more great experiences ahead. I doubt Boston was my last race; there are other marathons on my runner's bucket list – too many, in fact, to list here. Running has taught me that much is within my grasp as long as I am prepared to do the work required to seize it. And chasing Boston has been one of the most challenging and rewarding journeys of my life. For the first time in a long time, however, I'm in no hurry to get to a race, and especially not to finish it.

Would I like to back to Boston? Of course. There will never be another first time, but the experience was simply too good not to aspire to do it again. Some classic films are worth seeing repeatedly, even after you know every minute of the plot, including the ending.

But the obstacles are great and the price is high. For me, Boston will never be a routine, nor simply a decision. I'm not one of those runners who can count on getting in whenever he likes, running it every single year if he so chooses. I won't soon be finishing a race with ten minutes to spare on my qualifying time. Getting there the first time took me almost to the limit of my capacity. It was demanding on my time, my body, and my family. It took several years and four serious attempts. I'm not sure I'm ready to go through all of that, including the disappointment of failing, all over again, at least not any time soon.

Like most runners, I believe I have another fast marathon in my legs. At the right time, I'd welcome the chance to train hard again, to feel the satisfaction of completing a challenging long run or rising to meet the test in a series of demanding intervals. I love feeling spent but gratified.

So, if there is a chance of going back in a few years, if it's within my reach again, it seems unlikely I could resist another attempt.

But even if I were to devote another year or two to training and qualifying, there are no guarantees. It's reasonable to think the qualifying threshold will only get tougher, the bar raised even higher. One year after my Boston experience, runners had to surpass their qualifying times by almost two-and-a-half minutes. The time that got me into the 2015 Boston Marathon wouldn't have been good enough for 2016.

In another few years, will they bump the times up by another five minutes? Will I need to get even faster? Will an increase in demand for Boston offset any advantage I achieve by entering another age group? Will the inevitable decline in performance that comes with aging take away precious minutes? In other words, will time, my persistent nemesis, get the better of me again?

In a few years, perish the thought, I could be injured. Or I could simply be too slow. Or perhaps my motivation will be altered, even slightly, by the simple fact that I have already done it once. Going back to Boston is a little bit less compelling than getting there the first time.

If this was my only Boston Marathon, though, I can more than live with that. I survived all those Aprils when people were setting off for Boston and leaving me behind with my envy. I can manage a few more, knowing I've been there, done that, and gotten both the t-shirt and the jacket.

I'll never be able to predict the future, but I can always relish the past. In a marathon and in life, time can slip through your fingers. You can't change your bygone mistakes or failures, but nor can you erase your achievements. Just as irreversible as the many races I took too long to finish is the one occasion when I didn't. When I at last vanquished time in Pennsylvania, the result was permanent, irrevocable, etched in concrete or recorded in Wikipedia, depending on your generation. Time always marches on – in the end, it always wins. But when you cross a finish line, at least one clock stops forever.

Likewise, my long-awaited victory lap that began in Hopkinton the following spring is everlasting. You can no more take back a marathon from a runner than put a butterfly back in its cocoon. Boston is now a permanent chapter in my life story.

Michael Collins, a member of the Apollo 11 crew along with Neil Armstrong and Buzz Aldrin, once said in an interview that the moon sometimes surprises him. "I'll be out at night and I'll see a nice moon, and say, 'Hey, that looks good.' Then I'll say, 'Oh s---, I went up there one time!'" Likewise, every once in a while, on a run or in my car or in the shower, I'll think to myself, *Hey, I actually did it. I qualified. I ran the Boston Marathon.*

If I never go back, I'll always have April 20, 2015. I'll always have the lasting benefit of a long journey shared with a cherished friend, a trip of a lifetime with my beloved wife, a road that stretches back some 10,000 miles, through countless training runs and a score of marathons that all led to one finish line.

I'll always have the soundtrack of a twenty-six-mile course in my mind, the shoes hitting the ground, the water stations and the magnificent volunteers, the rising and fading music and the persistent exaltations of the spectators. If I never travel those streets again on foot, on a moment's notice I can go back there in my mind.

I'll always have Boylston Street. I'll always have the last few hundred yards, the crowd, the finish line, the emotional medal presentation from my new friend, the glorious hobbled march through the finish area and the embrace of my wife at the corner of Arlington Street.

I'll always have the wee hours of April 21, 2015, when I awoke at 3:45 and couldn't sleep again, my legs aching and my mind buzzing, and I felt both exhaustion and satisfaction. I'll always have the powerful lesson of meeting a difficult goal, of doing something tough, of climbing a summit because it's there, of seeing my friend Bob turn onto the high school track in Pennsylvania and knowing we'd made it, of discovering that meeting a worthwhile and longstanding objective isn't just ticking a box, it's reinforcing and even redefining who you are.

No matter what happens now, whether or not I go back, whether I ever run another marathon, whether I'm shuffling along at ninety or felled by injuries in my fifties, whether I live a long, healthy life or never take another step, wherever I go and whatever I do, I'll always have the one run I dreamed of and strived for, the triumph of having earned a place in the world's most coveted marathon, and the joy of having completed it. I'll always have Boston.

# CHAPTER 58

When I talk about running, or completing a marathon, or qualifying for Boston, some people respond by saying, "I could never do that." But neither could I, only a few years ago.

There are many things that are utterly impossible for most of us, but a marathon isn't one of them. Only a precious few are capable of becoming the explorers who climb mountains or venture into rarely traveled parts of the world, the heroes with limbs lost to war or cancer who run or cycle across the country for charity, the adventure athletes who traverse deserts or polar islands, the Olympians who destroy world records. Ordinary mortals like us may be inspired by these feats, but for the most part, all we can do is stand on the sidelines and applaud.

These superhuman figures may share some rare qualities and genetics that render them both physically and psychologically able both to attempt and achieve these remarkable deeds. But there are few distinct characteristics that separate the people at the finish line of a marathon from everyone else in the world, apart from the fact that they made the decision to get to the start line.

If politics is the art of the possible, running is the act of it. There's no doubt that a marathon is a remarkable achievement. But if there's one lesson to be learned from witnessing the wide range of people who have accomplished it, people of all shapes and sizes, ages and backgrounds, it's that no matter how daunting the distance and time, a marathon route is the well-traveled territory of ordinary people. What distinguishes them from everyone else is simply that they have chosen to do something extraordinary.

Almost every ability or skill we possess is something of which we were once incapable. We aren't born being able to walk, much less drive a car through highway traffic. But we cross those thresholds and more, one careful step at a time, over long, protracted periods of trying and failing, learning and then trying again. I've absorbed many lessons watching my kids grow from helpless blobs into (mostly) functional school-aged children. Few milestones are easily or quickly reached, but with patience and persistence, eventually you can get the result you desire.

Indeed, we gain none of these important proficiencies overnight. Our most important abilities are not achieved through a Hail Mary pass or a stroke of luck or genius. They are, like training for a marathon, a slog. You don't get a proper education in one week. You don't raise a child in one month. You don't get promoted to CEO on your first day out of college.

So unless there are specific medical issues that limit a person from doing the training, I quickly reject anyone who says, "I could never run a marathon." If you start putting one foot in front of another and follow a good training program, you might surprise yourself in six to twelve months. It might even take longer than that, but it's highly unlikely you'll do it in less time.

You know the expression, "It's a marathon, not a sprint"? It actually applies to running and not just life. The true endurance test of a marathon isn't whether you can get from the start to the finish, but whether you can get to the start.

But just because almost anyone can run a marathon doesn't diminish how remarkable it is when someone does. Running is no more original than many other special things in life: education, marriage, parenthood, and career. Indeed, like life itself, running a marathon isn't special because no one has ever done it before. It's special because you haven't.

For me, the passage to Boston is not about marathons or running. It's about validation – it's saying that you can cross the bridge from unable to able, that no matter how overwhelming and distant a goal may appear, you can get closer to it by taking one small step at a time.

There are many such goals that people attack every day. A marathon is just one example, one that I think happens to be very powerful and gratifying. Unlike so many other aspects of life for which success is subjective and ambiguous, a race with a finish line is clear and measurable.

Whatever the goal, my only advice is, go after it. Be methodical. Be patient. And above all, enjoy the journey and all of its life-affirming benefits. While my objective was to run Boston, the race itself was just a victory lap. The experience of chasing it was the greatest reward.

Whether or not we enter the Boston Marathon, we all have our Hopkintons. And we all have our Boylston Streets. There is great joy in the pursuit of both starts and finishes.

## APPENDIX 1

# TWENTY-SIX WORDS FOR TWENTY-SIX MILES

I asked runners to define, in twenty-six words or less, why Boston is the most coveted marathon in the world.

*"Sure, the physically challenging route – downhill to start, into hills later – but the crowds, the crowds! And the mass of humanity just running down a road."*

**LAUREL A. JOHNSON**

*"The best view is after the hardest climb. Qualifying is hard, hence most desired. Advice: Get faster or get older."*

**BENZION-CASPI**

*"I run marathons for the beer. Boston has Samuel Adams."*

**SHELDON BETTS**

*"Four months of training for the Boston Marathon in hot and cold weather is character building. Running on Patriots' Day through eight quaint towns: amazing!"*

**HILDA BEAUREGARD**

*"The Boston marathon is the victory lap to celebrate all the work it took to get there. The whole city welcomes runners for this joyful celebration."*

**PETER CHAPMAN**

*"Marathoner's prize: to toe the line with the best age-groupers on a course that challenges and torments, sustained by a proud chorus of a million cheerleaders."*

**PETER STAPLETON**

*"The Boston Marathon is the pinnacle of the sport...
and nobody rides for free!"*

**ANDY SHELP**

*"The Boston Marathon is sacred running ground. Qualify and you get to run through history in the footsteps of legends like Johnny Kelly and Bill Rodgers."*

**TIM SCAPILLATO**

*"I pursued Boston for the history, support, atmosphere and as a celebration of all that training (and of course I want one of those jackets)."*

**NEALE CHISNALL**

*"Physically and mentally challenging, inspiring, motivating, exciting, friendship-building, camaraderie, amazing spectators, fabulous expo, well organized and well supported."*

**CHERYL LEVI**

*"The only marathon with 26.2 miles of the loudest, proudest and most amazing spectators. The famous mile-long shrills from Wellesley College are a goose-bump-giving, once-in-a-lifetime experience."*

**DARCIA KMET**

APPENDIX 2

# SELECTED STATISTICS ABOUT THE BOSTON MARATHON

Total number of Boston Marathon registrants from 1897 to 2016: 647,309
Number of registrants from 1897 to 1967: 11,962
Number of registrants from 1968 to 2016: 635,347
Number of Boston Marathon registrants in 1897: 18
First year registration broke 100: 1906 (105)
First year registration broke 200: 1928 (285)
First year registration broke 300 and 400: 1964 (403)
First year registration broke 1,000: 1968 (1,014)
First year registration broke 2,000: 1975 (2,395)
First year registration broke 5,000: 1979 (7,927)
Number of registrants in the 99th Boston Marathon in 1995: 9,416
Number of registrants in the 100th Boston Marathon in 1996: 38,708
Number of registrants in the 101st Boston Marathon in 1997: 10,471
Number of registrants in the 2014 Boston Marathon, one year after the bombings: 35,755
Number of female registrants from 1972 to 2016: 211,412
Percentage of female participants in 1972: 0.7
Percentage of female participants in 2016: 45.9
Number of people named Mark who ran the 2015 Boston Marathon: 244
Number who finished ahead of the author: 149
Number of times Dick and Rick Hoyt ran the Boston Marathon: 32
Approximate number of Boston Marathon charity partners: 146

Estimated total amount raised for charity at the Boston Marathon since 1989: $234,000,000
Estimated amount raised in 2013: $20,000,000
Estimated amount raised in 2014, one year after the bombings: $38,400,000

# ACKNOWLEDGEMENTS

I'm indebted to a number of people who faithfully and generously supported me with time and energy, guidance and feedback about all aspects of this book, especially Mark Sullivan, Ben Kaplan, John Robson and Alex Hutchinson.

Thanks to the team of people who worked on the project, including the brilliant artist Sarah Lazarovic, who illustrated the cover, designer extraordinaire Tanya Connolly-Holmes, my colleagues at Great River Media, Terry Tyo and Michael Curran, and my editor, lifelong friend and *Reach for the Top* teammate, Kel Pero, who witnessed many of the events I describe from my sedentary youth.

I'm grateful for the community of runners who always both encourage and inspire me. I'm especially thankful to have shared this Boston experience with my great friend and the godfather of my children, Bob Plamondon.

My parents didn't inspire me to take up running, but they did encourage me to pursue my dreams and have always supported me every step of the way. Above all, I'm blessed to have at my side for every journey in life my best friend and cherished wife Ginny and our children Erica, Jack and Kate, who give me reasons to move faster and try harder every day.

# PRAISE FOR WHY I RUN

Here's what readers are saying in online reviews of *Why I Run: The Remarkable Journey of the Ordinary Runner.*

"I loved this book. I think it would appeal to all runners, whether you are running a 5k for the first time or have run fifty-plus marathons."

"This is an incredibly funny and inspiring read. Any runner will relate (and laugh out loud) at the wonderful stories within. It made me want to put on my running shoes and hit the road. Highly recommend this to all runners and athletes! You will not be disappointed!"

"I've read a few running books, but *Why I Run* is by far the best running book I've ever read! I was either smiling from ear to ear, crying because I was so touched by a story or laughing out loud because I could totally relate. This book captures what it feels like to be a runner and the joy, ecstasy, dedication and yes, sometimes pain of training for a race from start to finish. If you're a runner or you know someone who is, get this book. I promise you, it will be your favorite running book. This book will move you...literally."

"What a great read! As a newbie runner I found all the chapters and anecdotes truly inspirational."

"I found this book inspiring, entertaining and informative. To me there was a comfort in reading his take on racing and training because he talked about many of the same things I've experienced in my own racing and training but said them so much more eloquently than I ever could. I highly recommend this book if you are a runner."

"A hard book to put down, loaded with inspirational stories for the runner and non-runner alike. It's about running, but also about life. Highly recommended."

The ebook of *Why I Run: The Remarkable Journey of the Ordinary Runner* is available on all platforms.

EXCERPT FROM

# WHY I RUN: THE REMARKABLE JOURNEY OF THE ORDINARY RUNNER

I don't know when it will be. I don't know why it will be. But someday, there will be a last run.

When I started jogging around the neighborhood, even when I trained for my first marathon, I wasn't certain how long I would keep running. Maybe after a time, or having crossed a finish line and checked it off my list, I would switch to another activity.

But once the repetition engrains it into your lifestyle, rewires it into your DNA, it becomes hard to imagine not running. Today I dread even the idea of an injury sidelining me for a few months. I picture myself going stir crazy watching other people still running blissfully by while I wait out a recovery.

So the prospect of giving it up permanently is something I push to the farthest corner of my mind, the place for those topics that are especially hard to confront, like *Which of the Two of Us Will Die First?* or *Colonoscopies*.

But it must be so. Everything has a beginning and an end, and there will come a day when I will never run again.

I stop short of saying that one day I will no longer be a runner, because I like to think that even when I'm not running, I'm still a runner. No matter when you retire, can you ever stop being a coalminer or a soldier? Once something becomes part of your life, it remains etched in your character even if you let it lapse from your routine.

I wonder sometimes what specifically will make me stop. Though it's hard to picture now, it's possible I may just give it up. Maybe due to a variety of factors my running will dwindle over a few years and one day I just won't be doing it anymore. That must happen to a lot of runners. The motivation slips a little, you grow a little older. Maybe you take up another sport. But before you know it, you haven't been for a run in weeks. Then it's months, then years.

It could be that I get injured and never recover well enough to run again. I could get warned off running by a doctor. I could get sick.

And there is another possibility to consider: Will it be my last run because my life, not my running, gets interrupted? Like everyone else, runners die for more reasons than just old age or prolonged illness. Sometimes it happens suddenly. No matter what it does to improve our cardiovascular system and delay this and forestall that, running offers no guarantees.

I'm optimistic I'll be running in my fifties. But what about my sixties? The numbers, at least in terms of race participation, seem to drop off significantly there. Will I be one of those rare people still running when I'm seventy? Shuffling along at eighty? Even if I'm blessed with extraordinary luck and health, at some point it must end.

And before it does, there will be one last run.

Unless I feel a tweak or a twinge that day that leads to something serious, or I plan my retirement like some professional athlete on a farewell tour, it's more likely than not that I won't know it's my last run until much later. In all probability it will be a routine run, nothing out of the ordinary.

It goes without saying that I want that run to be as far in the future as possible. But more important than the timing, I want it to be a certain kind of run.

About once or twice a month, usually in the final mile as I head for home, for just a few moments I think about what I'm doing. I think about the air I'm breathing, the movement of my legs and the feeling of good health I get from a respectable run.

It often happens at a time when I've had to deal with something frustrating or unexpected. For maybe the only time that day, I'm living in the moment, enjoying what it feels like to throw one foot in front of the other, just as a child might.

I pick up the pace a little and feel a little bit of pride that despite a busy life, I've managed to stay in decent shape, good enough that I can head out the door on any given day and run for an hour or more without stopping.

And that gives me peace. And hope. And energy.

I pray that it isn't soon. But no matter when it is, I want the last run to be this kind of run.

As the final turn approaches, I think to myself, not everything in running and life is as I wish it to be. But it could be a lot worse.

After all, I'm alive and I'm running.